ALSO BY JERÉ LONGMAN

*The Girls of Summer: The U.S. Women's Soccer
Team and How It Changed the World*

*Among the Heroes: United Flight 93 and
the Passengers and Crew Who Fought Back*

*If Football's a Religion, Why Don't We Have a Prayer?: Philadelphia,
Its Faithful, and the Eternal Quest for Sports Salvation*

The Hurricanes: One High School Team's Homecoming After Katrina

Not Without Hope

NICK SCHUYLER
AND
JERÉ LONGMAN

HARPER

NEW YORK ● LONDON ● TORONTO ● SYDNEY

HARPER

A hardcover edition of this book was published in 2010 by William Morrow, an imprint of HarperCollins Publishers.

NOT WITHOUT HOPE. Copyright © 2010 by Nick Schuyler. All rights reserved. Printed in the United States of America. No part of this book may be used or reproduced in any manner whatsoever without written permission except in the case of brief quotations embodied in critical articles and reviews. For information address HarperCollins Publishers, 10 East 53rd Street, New York, NY 10022.

HarperCollins books may be purchased for educational, business, or sales promotional use. For information please write: Special Markets Department, HarperCollins Publishers, 10 East 53rd Street, New York, NY 10022.

FIRST HARPER PAPERBACK PUBLISHED 2011.

Library of Congress Cataloging-in-Publication Data has been applied for.

ISBN 978-0-06-199398-5

11 12 13 14 15 OV/RRD   10 9 8 7 6 5 4 3 2 1

In memoriam:

Will Bleakley
Marquis Cooper
Corey Smith

Not Without Hope

Prologue

I could not have my mother come to my funeral. A year later, that is the best explanation I can give. Four of us went into the water, and I was the only one who came out. Why me? My friends were just as big and strong and tough and brave. Two of them, Marquis Cooper and Corey Smith, played in the National Football League. Will Bleakley, my best friend, had been a tight end in college. We were young and athletic, and athletes grow to feel invincible. Yet I was the only one pulled from the Gulf of Mexico when our boat capsized. Why did I make it when they did not? It haunts me.

I think about that day, those horrible hours, all the time. The littlest thing puts me back out there: a stray thought, a glimpse of open water, a look from a stranger that says, "Aren't you that guy?" The accident trails me like the wake of Marquis's boat, churning, foaming, pushing toward the horizon of every day. Why me? Why did I make it when they did not? Science might have an answer in warm air trapped against the skin and sustained core body temperature, but that is a cold, clinical explanation. The only answer I have is my mother. I could not bear for her to see me in a casket, her twenty-four-year-old son laid out in waxy eternity—or even worse, lost forever at sea.

I am no hero. Maybe if I had brought my friends back with me. At least one of them . . . or all of them. But I didn't. I tried; I gave it everything I had, but I couldn't. I'm only a survivor. I was not particularly interested in telling my story. But I knew that someone would, and it might as well be me. I could deal in fact, not rumor. I could let the families of Marquis and Corey and Will know the truth of what happened. I could dispel the misinformation that we were horsing around and fighting and getting drunk. I could dismiss the ridiculous notion that they gave up or that I harmed them or ignored them to save myself. There is so much crazy stuff out there—I even heard somewhere that we were captured by pirates. In the end, I decided to write this book. It is cathartic to tell the story, though really that's the least of it. For the other families, I wanted the story to be told the right way, not so much for me but for them. And who knows? Maybe this story will help others avoid the mistakes we made.

This is the way I remember it. If I get some things wrong, it is due to the frailties of memory and the horror of what I experienced, not any intention to amend or deceive. This is what I recall after being in the water for forty-three hours, frigid and aching and scared, so hungry and thirsty that I felt I was eating my teeth. This is the best I can do after having three friends die, two of them in my arms. The saddest thing about this story is, I am the only one left to tell it.

Part I

The sun was not yet up when we put into the water on February 28, 2009. It was about six thirty on a Saturday morning, and nearly a dozen boats had already launched from the Seminole Boat Ramp in Clearwater, Florida. Their lights shined green and red. Residential towers lined the Intracoastal Waterway. A few hundred yards ahead stood the Causeway Bridge that separated downtown Clearwater from Clearwater Beach. There was wind in the palm trees at the boat launch. Sometimes a gust seemed to brush the shallow water like suede. A cold front was expected to blow through later in the day.

Clearwater, located west of Tampa on Florida's Gulf Coast, is the home of the original Hooters. Says so right on the building. It is also the spring training base of the Philadelphia Phillies, who had won the World Series a few months earlier. Players had reported to camp for another expectant season, but there was still a chill in the air in late winter. We were bundled up in jackets and hats and windbreakers and wind pants. I ran my hand through the water, and it felt cold. Don't worry, Marquis said. It would warm up by the time we stopped to catch our bait fish.

We were headed about sixty-five or seventy miles west of Clearwater Pass to a shipwreck site that was one of Marquis's favorite fishing areas. In a week, he was leaving town for an off-season training camp with the Oakland Raiders. He had sold his house and was closing in a few days. Most of his furniture was already out. He was scheduled to fly to Seattle, where he had attended the University of Washington. He would pick up a car and drive down to Oakland for minicamp. This fishing trip was a going-away celebration. Marquis planned to keep a residence in the Tampa area, but he wasn't sure if he would get another chance to fish before football season started. He loved being on the water. He spent all his free time with his family or his boat. He had met his wife, Rebekah, at Washington. They had a three-year-old daughter, Delaney. He called her Goose.

Marquis was twenty-six, and had been drafted by Tampa Bay in the third round of the 2004 NFL draft. He had played for six teams, including three stints with the Pittsburgh Steelers. He was undersized for a linebacker at 6 feet 3 inches, 215 pounds. But Marquis was a freak of nature—the strongest pound-for-pound guy I have ever seen. Maybe 6 percent body fat. Absolutely shredded, ripped. Skinny waist, real skinny torso, giant shoulders and back. He looked like he weighed 230 because he was so thin and so wide.

Marquis was cool, calm, and collected. He stuttered a bit, but he had a swagger about him. Real nice guy. We met at an L.A. Fitness where I worked as a personal trainer in Lutz, Florida, just north of Tampa. You could tell he was somebody special, not just another guy working out. We got close around New Year's of 2009. I saw how he worked out and how good a shape he was in. I would give him a hard time. I told him I could push him, get him to another level.

"You need to start working with me," I told him.

Sure, why not? he said. He was having trouble gaining weight.

"I do need someone to push me," he said.

Oakland had signed Marquis for the last half of the 2008 season and for 2009. Twice in eight games in 2008, he had been awarded the game ball for his play on special teams. He was smooth, elegant, a little quiet at first until he opened up. Working with him was a way for me to get into better shape as he became more fit. And to be honest, it was a way to show off, to show him what I could do.

That first week, we worked so hard lifting that he got sick almost every day. Threw up. He was drinking some kind of weight-gain shake, and it was tearing him up. We were lifting heavy weights continuously, working out ninety minutes or two hours, the longest break a minute, just boom, boom, boom. Soon he got into ridiculous shape. He would squat 405 pounds in sets of eight, and bench 315 pounds in sets of eight. He was the only person who could beat me at this one drill I devised—three push-ups and one pull-up, ten repetitions as fast as you could. He could do it in fifty-one seconds. My best was fifty-seven seconds. He was fast, very quick. He could dunk a basketball like it was nothing. He always found a way to win when we played H-O-R-S-E. He had an ugly stroke, but the ball went in.

If there was any sport he loved as much as football, it was fishing. He grew up in the desert, in Phoenix, but he was drawn to the water around the University of Washington campus in Seattle. In college, he kept pets—Hoss, a pit bull; Red, a red-tailed boa constrictor; and Vic Damone Jr., a python named after the alias Chris Tucker's character used in the movie *Money Talks*. He still kept dogs, Boston terriers named Hercules, Dori, and Winston. He also had a fish pond that seemed to be ten feet deep in his backyard, filled with fish, some of which he had caught himself.

Fishing and football and his family meant everything to Marquis. After football, Marquis planned to make fishing his second career. He would become a captain and run his own charter business. He said he felt calm and peaceful on his boat. And he was terrific at fishing. He thought that being a charter captain would be fun, like football. It wouldn't feel like work or be as stressful as an ordinary job. He once told the *San Francisco Chronicle,* "I used to go freshwater, but now I'm salt and that's it. Don't show me no lake, river, or nothing. It's a drug. You get hooked. You need it, like you want a new pole or you want new reels. I just go out there and get it done."

I had also met Corey at the gym a couple months earlier. He was 6 feet 3 inches, 265 pounds, 12 percent body fat. You can look at people and tell they're unique. I knew he was some kind of athlete when I noticed his pants or his gloves or something bore the logo of the NFL. Like Marquis, Corey was undersized. As a defensive end, he sometimes played against tackles who outweighed him by sixty or seventy pounds. He had gone undrafted out of North Carolina State in 2002, but caught on with Tampa Bay as a free agent. He played in six of the first nine games in 2002, then finished the season on injured reserve, unable to play in the Super Bowl as the Buccaneers defeated the Raiders. I'm not sure if Corey got a Super Bowl ring; if he did, he was modest about his accomplishments—I didn't see him wear it. Still, against long odds, he had built a nice career for himself. Briefly, he and Marquis played together with the Buccaneers in 2004, but I don't think they had known each other well.

Corey's career had been one of extremes. He played on a Super Bowl team as a rookie, and in 2008 he played on a Detroit Lions team that lost all sixteen of its games. But he was known as a durable, reliable backup. In high school in Richmond, Virginia, Corey was so relentless on the field that his nickname was the Tasmanian Devil. He played the same way in the pros. The Lions loved to talk about a play from the 2007 season. Corey had a strained hamstring muscle, and the Detroit coaches tried to replace him on the kickoff return team in a game against Chicago.

"Coach, I can give you one more play," Corey told Stan Kwan, the Lions' special teams coach. "I might not be able to walk after that, but I can give you one more play."

So they left him in the game. The Bears tried an onside kick, but the Lions recovered. Corey made two blocks on the return, sprung his teammate for a touchdown, and the Lions won. While everyone else celebrated the touchdown, Corey limped to the sideline. He was finished for the day, but he had done his job. The next day, Rod Marinelli, Detroit's head coach at the time, showed a replay of Corey's blocks to the team as a sign of determination and toughness.

"Rod just showed the play over and over," Kwan told the *Detroit News*. "Right then and there, his teammates knew he was a team guy first. He's not the fastest guy. He wasn't the tallest or biggest guy for a defensive end, but his heart was bigger than everybody else's."

Corey became a free agent after the 2008 season, but he seemed confident that he would catch on with a team by training camp, maybe even in the next month.

"Are you worried?" I asked him.

"I'll be fine," he said.

He could be quiet and serious, until he opened up. He was curious. He wanted to hear stories from you more than the other way around. But he had a great, loud laugh. And if you said something he didn't quite believe, he would give you a grinning, sarcastic, "Whaaaat?"

Corey had a sweet tooth for brownies and ice cream, had tried yoga, knew how to juggle, tinkered with computers, and, unlike many superstitious athletes, deliberately avoided pregame routines. He once told the *Grand Rapids Press*, "I have an antiroutine. I try to do something different before every game."

I was training Marquis, and I told Corey, "You need to come work out with us." The three of us were pretty much together four days a week, if not five. We would probably put in twenty-plus hours together, working out, having lunch. They were great guys to hang out with. And it got me in great shape, too.

I asked them about their workouts in the NFL, and they said it was just basic lifting, all power lifts designed for pure strength. We did a lot combination exercises besides the regular bench, squat, and leg press. We did auxiliary lifts, side raises, curls, shrugs, and lunges, trying to build stamina, endurance, conditioning. I was trying to drop their body fat and put muscle on them at the same time. They both got a whole lot of gains. Corey's bench press went up 25 pounds in three months: He was benching eight reps of 335 pounds. Corey didn't drink alcohol. Not an ounce. He and Marquis always talked about other players, coaches, people they had in common. After the NFL, I think Corey wanted to get into coaching. I never heard him say a bad word about anyone.

They would laugh at some of my routines. I'd put four plates on the bar and do a set of ten Romanian dead lifts—bending at the waist, legs slightly bent but locked, back flat, butt out—and lift 405 pounds to my waist. That hurts. It's a lot of weight, particularly on your spine. They looked at me like why would anybody want to put that much stress on their body? We got into a groove and worked hard, and they made a lot of gains. Then it was almost time for Marquis to head out West. Before he left, he wanted to take us fishing.

A week earlier, Corey and I had gone along on Marquis's boat, to the same place we were headed today. I didn't know much about deep-sea fishing. Nothing, in fact. I had grown up in Chardon, Ohio, outside of Cleveland. When I was young, my mother would take me to a park, and I'd walk to the end of the dock and drop a line. You could see the bluegills and sunfish. You would literally drop the worm and put it to their face. So this deep-sea business was basically new to me. I had gone out only once, off Virginia Beach, when I was seven years old. I don't even think I cast my line once. I just threw up all day. With Marquis and Corey, I was just along for the ride.

Marquis kept saying, "I'll take you out fishing. You need to come. Your whole body will be sore after a day of fishing. It's a good feeling, a different kind of sore from working out."

And fishing meant going out to the Gulf of Mexico—more than fourteen thousand feet at its deepest point. The Gulf produces a quarter of the United States' natural gas and an eighth of its oil. It also provides some of the world's most abundant fisheries. By the beginning of the decade, about 20 percent of the nation's commercial fish and shellfish were harvested from the Gulf, along with 40 percent of the country's recreational finfish. The world's largest fish—whale sharks, which grow to fifty feet—were also being spotted in the Gulf in record numbers. They were apparently attracted by plankton blooms fed by fertilizer and other nutrients flowing from the Mississippi River. Fish, shrimp, and squid were also drawn to the cooler, plankton-rich waters that upwelled along the continental shelf off of Florida.

Corey and I could not figure out why Marquis loved fishing. It was so much work. The weekend before, we got to Marquis's house at four thirty in the morning and were on the water by six fifteen. We went more than seventy miles out. He would catch a fish every five minutes: red snapper, grouper, lemon sharks, amberjacks. Corey and I didn't know what to do with the poles or how to get the fish off the hook or put the bait on. Marquis would laugh at us.

"Y'all are worthless!" he said.

Then he would say, "Hold on," and stop what he was doing and get us set up. Then he would start fishing again—and every time he cast his line, he seemed to pull up a fish.

He would try to tell us how to tie certain knots, and we were like, "Yeah, whatever, dude. Can you help us get this fish off our hook?"

I caught my first fish and I was like, oh my God, forget this. I was so confused. Why would anybody like this? It took me almost fifteen minutes to get the damn fish up. A big amberjack. As soon as I made a little leeway, it yanked out everything I had reeled in. It fought like a shark. My back and shoulders were burning. I kind of wedged the pole between my legs and told Marquis, "I'm taking a little break." I couldn't imagine anyone pulling up a giant marlin or something.

"Pull, pull!" Marquis kept yelling at me and laughing. By then, he had probably already caught five fish.

It was choppy on the ride back that first time, and we were going thirty-five miles an hour. Corey and I kept saying, "How much longer, how much longer?" We were ready for it to be over. When we finally got back to the dock, Corey and I got in Marquis's truck while he and a friend iced the fish and cleaned the boat. I was so tired and hungry and cold. We were wet. We smelled.

"No way in hell we're doing this again," Corey and I said to each other.

We didn't get home until ten. Two nights later, we got together and grilled and fried some of the snapper, the shark, the amberjack, and the grouper. I don't like fish. I don't like the smell or the texture or the taste. They kept giving me a hard time.

"You gotta try it," Marquis would say, laughing. "You're such a bitch. Don't be a bitch. It's so much better fresh. Trust me."

Finally, I tried it. It wasn't bad. I was surprised. Not that I was going to go out to a seafood restaurant any time soon.

Marquis was so happy that night. We played Rock Band, the video game, and he kept telling his young daughter, Delaney, "Inside voice, inside voice," until she put on this one song and began screaming into the mike and we all started laughing. All of a sudden, he was telling her, "Louder, louder!" It was the cutest thing.

Before he left for Oakland, Marquis wanted to go out fishing one more time.

"I don't know," I tried to tell him, but he kept saying, "Come on, I may not get a chance to go out again until this time next year."

Corey and I debated it.

"All right, we'll do it," we said. "Why not?"

Any time I got to spend with those guys was fun.

Marquis's boat had a capacity of ten people, but he never wanted more than four aboard, especially with guys as big as we were and the distance we were going out. He had a twenty-one-foot boat, with the helm located at a center console under a small canopy. It was powered by a two-hundred horsepower, single-engine outboard motor. Fuel capacity was sixty-six gallons. For extra fuel, we had five five-gallon cans of gas bungeed at the stern.

A friend of Corey's, a former teammate named Chuck Darby, was supposed to make this trip with us today, but he had been uncertain during the week. I called my best friend, Will Bleakley, and told him not to get his hopes too high, but there might be room for him if the other guy dropped out. On Thursday, two days before the trip, Chuck canceled. He had to go to South Carolina to visit his father, who was ill. I called Will.

"Keep your plans open," I told him.

Friday morning, Marquis was busy getting his house together for his move out West. He texted me that he couldn't work out at the gym, but he invited Will on the trip: "Tell your boy it's all good. He can come."

Will had expressed some concern to his parents. He didn't know Marquis and Corey and had never been deep into the Gulf. But he was a decisive person. Once he made his mind up, he wasn't one to second-guess. When I told him he could come along, he got superexcited. He texted me all day Friday: What should I bring? How much beer? What are we going to eat? Dude, I can't wait. Let's go to bed at eight tonight so we can get up early.

"Don't forget my jacket," I reminded him. I was going to be a lot better prepared on this trip than I had been last week. I was taking a jacket, gloves, sweatpants, a sweatshirt, and a skull cap. Marquis had advised us to bring something water-resistant. I had worn just a sweatshirt and sweatpants the first time, and I got drenched. Will had borrowed my winter jacket a couple months earlier. He went to New York City for New Year's. It was an L.L. Bean jacket, orange with black piping, doubled-lined, water-resistant on the outside, and fleece-lined on the inside. When I zipped up the front, I looked like a human pumpkin, but I didn't care. It kept me warm.

Will got to my house in Tampa at four on Friday afternoon, before I even got home from work. Not that I minded. We were inseparable, and he was over every weekend. Will had his own bedroom at the house, his own sofa in the living room. My girlfriend, Paula Oliveira, called him "our son." So did our friends. We'd go somewhere and they would inevitably ask, "You bringing your son?"

I think he got a kick out of it.

I was twenty-four; Will was a year older. I was 6 feet 2 inches, 239; he was 6 feet 3 inches, 230, brown hair, brown eyes—a ladies' man. Will had degrees in finance and accounting, but he had lost his job in the recession. He was thinking about going back to school. We had pictures of each other all over my house, usually taken at a party or a game or some other light moment. We were usually smiling, with an arm around each other, often holding a beer. From certain angles, with hair on our chins, we even looked somewhat alike. Will was my best friend, and he was Paula's best friend, too.

I used to tell Will that I wanted him to be my best man or a groomsman at my wedding, and Paula would say she wanted him to be the maid of honor. One of us would do something for him— cater to him or cook him something—and say, "Okay, Will, whose side you gonna stand on now?" He would never give us a straight answer.

We were together so often, we began to speak with the same sarcastic phrases: "You're right," or "I'm not just saying this" or one of us would make a rude comment and say, "Oh, did I say that out loud?" Will would catch himself and go, "Dammit." He was our designated puppysitter and dog walker, too. How good a job he did was another story.

Football brought Will and I together, just as football was at the intersection of my friendships with Marquis and Corey. Will played at the University of South Florida in Tampa from 2002 through 2006. He was a good student and a terrific athlete, a preferred walk-on. He considered the Coast Guard Academy and the Air Force Academy before deciding to stay close to home for school. He played in thirty-four games during his career, starting eight times at tight end and catching ten passes. I think he made honorable mention at All–Big East Conference his senior year. He was clever at chop blocking. His parents, Bob and Betty, were at the games, always.

I made the team as a walk-on in February 2006, before spring practice began. I had moved down to Tampa in August 2005 after spending two years at Kent State. My father has a painting business nearby, in Tarpon Springs, and I came down to help him. I wasn't too interested in school anymore. But I watched a couple of football games at the USF and thought I could play with those guys.

It had been five years since I played football. Even though I had lettered in football, I stopped after my sophomore year at Chardon High in Ohio to concentrate on basketball. The football coaches wanted me to show up for off-season training on the days we had basketball games. I didn't think that was right, so I chose basketball and made third team all-state, averaging fourteen and a half points and eleven and a half rebounds.

When I graduated from Chardon High in 2003 I thought about playing basketball at Kent State, but I tore the anterior cruciate ligament in my knee the summer after my senior year. During my sophomore year at Kent, I could feel myself kind of growing up. I continued to party and have fun, but I limited myself to three times a month instead of twice a weekend. I just decided I wanted a change, to do something while I was still young. I kept thinking, How can I do this? I decided that after my sophomore year, I would pick up and go.

Chardon was about thirty minutes outside of Cleveland, near Lake Erie, a small town in the snowbelt of northeast Ohio. We averaged more than 100 inches of snow a year. Sometimes, we'd have 5 feet of snow on the ground, and a wind chill of –30, and they'd have to call the National Guard to come in. But you get used to the cold if that's what you know. I used to sit outside in shorts when it was 25 degrees.

It was fun out there in the snow. I rode four-wheelers and was a daredevil snow skier. We lived near a church, and when they plowed the parking lot, we would take the snow mounds and make them into giant ramps. We would ski over the snow like we were on water skis: the four-wheeler would veer away at the last minute, and we would let go of the rope and do double back flips or 720s—two full helicopter spins. Other times we drove ten minutes to a small ski resort, Alpine Valley, and I used to jump off the lift from twenty feet in the air or pop off a ski on purpose and go down the hill on one leg. I always skied as fast as I could. Fun, stupid things.

I also loved following the local pro teams—the Browns, the Cavaliers, and the Indians. What I didn't love was the random weather. One day it would be 60 degrees, the next it would be 35 and raining and ugly, then 25 and snowing and then 45 and sunny. I loved the weather in Tampa. Compared to Ohio, it felt like a permanent vacation.

I got back into school in January 2006 and showed up for football tryouts at USF in February with 140 other guys. They asked 15 of us to stay around for winter conditioning, and then invited 8 of us back for spring ball. Will was a tight end heading into his senior year. I was on the defensive line, psyched about the opportunity to get back into the game.

I didn't have a whole lot of friends at school. I wasn't close to my roommates. One was a bookworm; the other worked a lot on his motorcycles. We didn't really go out or stuff like that. So I spent the fall of 2005 and all spring and summer of 2006 preparing for football.

I lifted weights and ate eight thousand calories a day to put on weight. I'd probably eat a dozen eggs a day and a pound of spaghetti and cookies every night. My girlfriend at the time loved it. She had a sweet tooth, and I was trying to put on some pounds. Then I'd go to sleep and wake up in the middle of the night and drink a massive weight-gain shake.

On the street outside my town house, I spray-painted markers for the forty-yard dash, the hundred-yard dash. I'd run ten times a hundred or fifteen times forty, with a one-minute break in between. Sometimes I'd fall asleep early and wake up at midnight and get out there and run in the dark.

I put on about 30 pounds. I was 250 when I made the team in the spring of 2006 and 276 at the start of fall training camp. I was in top shape. One of the coaches called me Big 'Roid. They thought I was on steroids. No way—I'm as anti-steroids as you can get. In the weight room, I was probably in the top five strengthwise in every lift.

Will and I weren't that close at the beginning. Like I said, Will was a tight end, and I was a defensive lineman. People don't realize it, but the offense and defense are often kept separate on teams. Sometimes there is even tension between them. They dress on different sides of the locker room, practice on different fields, and hang out with teammates who play similar positions. Despite that, eventually Will and I became friends. It turned out we lived close to each other, so we started riding together. I'd pick him up for football, or he'd pick me up. Then he started coming over for dinner. Eventually we got his mother's recipe for pasta. Betty's pasta, we called it, four kinds of cheese and bread crumbs. We loved it.

Will was a starter in 2006, his senior year. I was a junior, but my career ended before it began. The first week of the season I was inactive because I had an incomplete grade. The second week I was getting ready to run out of the tunnel with my uniform on when I got stopped. I literally had to take my pads off while everyone ran onto the field. I hadn't been cleared to play by the N.C.A.A. I was heartbroken. My family was there. They were so proud of me, and now I wouldn't get a chance to play. I was so embarrassed. I wanted to cry and kill someone at the same time.

Halfway through the next week, they told me I would have to sit out the entire 2006 season. Even though I had never played college football, I was ineligible for a year because I had transferred from Kent State. The coaches tried to see what they could do, but it was out of their hands. Why the school waited so long to tell me this, I don't know. I had been on the team since the previous February, and there had been talk of a possible scholarship. Now I had to wait a whole year. I guess that's what you get for being a walk-on. I stuck it out the next couple of weeks, practicing with the scout team, but you get treated like garbage when you're not eligible. I just couldn't do it. I decided to hang up my pads. I would have had one year of eligibility remaining in 2007, but I couldn't wait that long. It was one of the hardest decisions I ever had to make. I had trained six hours a day to make that team. When they told me I'd have to sit out a year, it felt almost as bad as season-ending surgery. That was tough. By now, the majority of my friends were on the team. They were busy playing ball, and I wasn't. It was kind of awkward. I distanced myself from them and just lay low.

I gave football one more shot in October 2008, as I was finishing my last semester at USF. This time I tried out for the Tampa Bay Storm, an indoor professional team in the Arena Football League. I quit drinking for four months, cut weight, and worked out ten times a week, lifting weights in the day and doing drills at night. I got down to 233 pounds, 6 percent body fat—real lean. In the end, that hurt me. I was among the top three fastest of the three hundred people who tried out, but I was underweight. They wanted guys who were 265, 270, to play both linebacker and fullback. It was frustrating, but in the end, I guess it wasn't meant to be—the whole league folded.

At the time, I was in about the best shape I've ever been in prior to training with Marquis and Corey. I really loved being a fitness trainer. Working out and lifting weights for me creates a way to relieve stress. I hold a lot of stuff inside, and this is a way to burn off my anxiety. Working out clears my mind, kind of levels me off. Some people enjoy shopping or have a drink or eat food for comfort. I enjoy working out. And I like working with other people. I'm hands-on in that way. One of the best feelings is seeing a person reach his or her goal, getting stronger, losing weight, feeling more self-confident.

Will didn't lift weights as much as he once did, but he still swam at a YMCA for an hour three times a week. We grew closer after he graduated from USF. He was from Crystal River, Florida, a small town of about 3,500 people located about an hour north of Tampa. It's on Kings Bay, which is spring-fed so that its temperature remains constant through the year. During the winter, nearly 400 manatees gather in the temperate waters. His parents lived on a channel. He loved to fish and was big into camping. In high school, he and his friends used to go on all-night shark fishing trips just off the coast. We played golf together, though he was much better than I was. If that wasn't bad enough, he deliberately refused to help me improve.

I would ask him, "Okay, seriously, how do I get better?"

"Stop sucking," he would say.

"How do I stop sucking?"

"Hit the ball straighter," he would say.

We always ended up having a few drinks when we played. I always got better after a few beers—at least, I thought I did.

We went camping quite a few times, up north toward Ocala. We'd hike and go canoeing. We hunted armadillos, gophers, and raccoons. Everything became a contest. We invented drinking games. We'd see who could make the cleanest, most difficult dive into the springs where we camped. Or who could make the cleanest and best-looking hobo pie—a combination of grilled cheese sandwich and pizza, made on two pieces of white bread with butter, cheese, sauce, and pepperoni, cooked over a fire. I always won.

At Easter 2007, we stayed in Tampa and turned that into a game, too. We had a weigh-in before dinner. Then for an hour, a few of us ate as much as we could to see who could put on the most pounds. I drank an entire gallon of milk to try to beat Will. I filled myself with ham, turkey, stuffing, mashed potatoes, sweet potatoes, green beans, corn, dinner rolls, and salad. I gained 5.9 pounds, but Will gained 6. I was so pissed. It was his first meal of the day and my third. "That's bullshit," I kept saying. We were so uncomfortably full. Then we slept for an hour, woke up, and ate homemade ice-cream cake.

We played on a couple of rec softball teams together, and we won every year. Will would go four for five with four home runs. In high school, he once hit a four-hundred-foot grand slam in a playoff game. The ball lodged in a pine tree and they started calling it Bleakley's Tree. "He didn't get named Will for nothing," Brent Hall, his high school coach, said. "He had the most will out of anybody I've ever met."

We played in a couple of volleyball leagues together and won a title in one of those, too. We got big into tailgating after football was done. We'd get to the stadium at eleven in the morning for a night game and play this game called cornhole, tossing bean bags through a hole cut into rectangular boxes—sort of like parking lot horseshoes. Will was unbeatable at that, too.

Friday night, as we got ready for the fishing trip, Will was like a kid on Christmas Eve. We made a dozen peanut-butter-and-jelly and turkey-and-cheese sandwiches on white bread, and wrapped them in foil. We had peanuts, pretzels, chips, water, thirty beers each for me, Will, and Marquis.

I had texted Marquis on Friday: "It's your last weekend. Don't worry. Corey doesn't drink. If worse comes to worst, he can drive the boat. We're bringing it all. We're gonna get rowdy."

"Make sure you buy me at least six Coronas," he replied.

I guess it was something about Corona and bottles and the beach and the water. He also wanted six crustless peanut-butter-and-jelly sandwiches.

"We'll see," Marquis said about letting Corey drive the boat. He didn't sound too convinced that it was a good idea.

Friday night, Will sat on his couch in my living room, making his sandwiches on the coffee table.

"Who do Marquis and Corey play for?" he wanted to know. "What positions do they play? Are they cool?"

Sure, I told him.

"How far out we going?"

This was really our first time fishing together.

"Seventy miles," I said.

"I've never been out that far."

"It's great," I told him. "You literally drop the hook and yank it a couple of times and you catch a fish."

Will had fished mostly inland or near the coastline. As he told stories about what he had caught, he seemed to Paula to be speaking a different language.

She kept joking with him.

"It's going to be so boring, so cold," she told Will.

He wasn't buying it.

"Paula, you just don't get it," he said. "I haven't done this in such a long time."

I went to bed at ten. Will still had the TV on. He was too geared up to turn in. He drank a rum and Coke and thought that might help him shut his eyes.

My sister, Kristen, also stayed at my house Friday night. She was running a 5K race Saturday morning and had driven up from Fort Myers. She took Will's room, and Will took a sofa in the living room. She got up at two in the morning to go to the bathroom, and Will still had the TV on.

"You should go to bed," Kristen told him.

"I can't," Will said. "I'm so excited."

WE AWOKE AT four—I had cereal and a protein bar—and we headed out the door fifteen or twenty minutes later. We loaded Will's truck with our gear, a cooler, grocery bags, and beer, and headed out for Marquis's house a half hour away.

Kristen got up at about the same time for her race. As we headed out the door, Kristen said, "Have fun, see you later. Love you." She told me that if she did well in her race, I'd have to go see her run the next one.

Corey arrived at Marquis's house five minutes before we did. I introduced Will to everyone. We were all tired, pretty quiet. Marquis had already hitched the boat and trailer to his Chevy Silverado pickup with its lifted suspension and oversize tires.

Marquis must have had fifty fishing rods, and from his garage he chose ten of them as carefully as a chef chooses his carving knives. He stood in the boat as we handed him the beer, food, and drinks. There was a pair of twenty-gallon coolers aboard, one in front of the center console, which held mostly beer, drinking water, and ice. A second cooler, located under the bench-shaped captain's chair, was filled with water, Gatorade, sandwiches, and protein bars. Both coolers were secured by bungee cords.

Into a storage area in the center console, we loaded a case of beer, paper towels, toilet paper, chips, and pretzels. Will handed me his cell phone and his wallet. I placed them in my backpack along with my phone and wallet, and tossed the backpack into the storage compartment where the life jackets were kept.

Before six, we were on our way. Marquis played rap music in his truck, not too loud, but loud enough that we had to talk over it. We stopped to gas up the boat. Marquis got a breakfast burrito, or something just as nasty, took a couple bites, and threw it away. By six twenty-one, we were at the Seminole Boat Ramp in Clearwater.

The weather was cool, and we were bundled up. I had my jacket, sweatshirt, and sweatpants on. Will wore a green wind jacket and wind pants from USF's appearance in the PapaJohns.com Bowl in 2006. Corey had on a black wind jacket and wind pants. Marquis wore purple wind pants from the University of Washington and a heavier black winter jacket.

Marquis had been monitoring the weather. A couple days earlier he had said that a cold front was approaching and that the water might get rough. If it did, we might cut our trip short. He said it again this morning: "I'm not sure if we'll go all the way out."

Everyone went to the bathroom at the marina. Will asked what we would do if we felt the urge while at sea. I told him what Marquis had told me a week earlier: "Hang over the side and hope the sharks don't bite your ass."

Corey and Marquis put their wallets, cell phones, and keys into a Ziploc bag. Marquis stored the bag in a compartment in the roof of the canopy, near the radio. He had a digital camera in the bag, too, which contained pictures from our previous trip. I showed them to Will and told Marquis for a second time to send me the pictures. We had become good friends, but I had no photos of him and me together.

A couple of minutes after we set off, Marquis, Will, and I cracked the first beer of the day. "Let's get this party rolling," I said.

Stu Schuyler, Nick's father, had awakened early in nearby Tarpon Springs, where he owned a painting business. He had gone back to sleep, then climbed out of bed again at seven. He turned on the television and saw that a forceful upper air disturbance was approaching the southeastern United States from the northwest. He had seen Corey and Nick two days earlier at the gym and they told him they were headed to the same spot they had fished the previous weekend.

About seven fifteen, Stu grabbed his cell phone.

"Nick, if you get this message, head back early," Stu said. "A big storm's coming in."

His call went directly to voice mail.

Part II

Obeying no-wake zones along the Intracoastal Waterway, we made our way slowly under the four-lane Causeway Bridge and the Gulf Boulevard Bridge into Clearwater Pass, which separates Clearwater Beach from the barrier island of Sand Key. To our right rose a series of white, pink, and coral residential towers. We could also see the blue-gray façade of Shephard's Beach Resort, with its beach bar and all-you-can-eat crab buffet. A vacant area was the former site of the Spyglass Hotel. Seven months earlier, Criss Angel had performed the illusion of surviving the hotel's implosion while shackled to a balcony. To our left was a ninety-five-acre park and beach along Sand Key. About a thousand yards ahead lay the open Gulf.

Before heading into open water, we stopped near a buoy to load up on bait fish. This was one of Marquis's hot spots. We dropped lures with five hooks, and within a few moments the lures seemed to be quivering with fish. It was windy; you could smell the salt air. Pelicans and seagulls hovered around the boat. "Who's winning the fish race now?" I bragged, as I kept count of the bait fish.

In a half hour, I had caught more than thirty of the tiny fish that would be the lure for much larger grouper, snapper, and amberjacks.

"I'm fine here," I joked. "Why do we have to leave?"

Everyone was laughing and having a good time.

About seven thirty, with our bait tank stocked, we entered the Gulf. A week earlier, Marquis drove about thirty-five miles an hour to the shipwreck site. Today it was choppy, and he had to slow down. We kept switching spots on the boat, trying to get comfortable as we bounced up and down. Will and I sat on the front cooler, but it felt like my brain was slapping against the top of my head. I tried to drink the beer I'd popped open, but the water was too rough: it foamed and spilled everywhere. We moved to the back of the boat, sitting on chairs on either side of the outboard motor, but water from the bait well splashed us, so we had to cover it with a towel. I felt the pounding in my butt and my back. I decided it would be better to stand and absorb the hammering with my legs.

We stopped five or six times on the way to the wreck site to drop a line or pee or grab a sandwich or just to take a break from the pounding. The sky looked like puffs of gray cotton balls. The seas ran about five or six feet, and the waves seemed to come randomly from all directions. You constantly had to grab on to something. If you weren't careful, you'd probably fly off. We struggled with the anchor. It wouldn't catch, or we wouldn't drop it properly, so we drifted downwind, and Marquis grew frustrated trying to position the boat near the schools that appeared on his fish finder.

Someone had warned me to take Dramamine to prevent seasickness, saying, "Once you get sick, you don't get better." Since I hadn't gotten sick the week before, I ignored them. Today was another story. Oh, shit, I thought to myself. I started feeling dizzy and warm, and my mouth got dry. I stopped eating the salted sunflower seeds we had brought along. I poured out my second beer. We had cases of the stuff, but nobody would be doing much drinking in this weather. I began spitting a lot. My stomach was turning. I knew it was going to be a long day. Marquis had already warned us, "If you get sick, too bad, I ain't turning around."

About eleven thirty in the morning, we reached our primary fishing spot, seventy-five miles west of Clearwater. The water was 150 feet deep at this point. Supposedly there was a shipwreck that served as an alluring artificial reef.

Will caught the first fish, a red snapper. He and Marquis seemed to attract snapper, grouper, and amberjack like a magnet attracts iron filings. We caught a few small lemon sharks. Marquis cut two of them open—I guess it was a way to preserve them for the trip home—and both times baby sharks spilled out.

WILL AND I told Marquis and Corey that we wanted to take them camping at some point. We explained how you go hunting and wake up with beer and eggs in front of the fire, clean up, and drink some more. Marquis started laughing.

"Okay, all right, I'm good," he said, though he didn't think that his wife, Rebekah, would come along.

Corey had his doubts about sleeping in the woods.

"I like my bed," he said. "I don't like bugs."

The waves began to settle in—still choppy, but not as random. They struck the boat with quick jolts, and it rocked from side to side. I took a wide stance—there was cushioning along the sides of the boat to help brace myself. But I kept having to take a break from fishing. I got more and more nauseous. The guys began to tease me.

"Suck it up."

"You better not be getting sick."

And when their admonitions failed, they said, "Dude, you don't look good."

Then I vomited. Everything came up: cereal and peanut butter and jelly and bread and pretzels—it was orange, thick, and sandy. Will began laughing hysterically.

We would drop two lines each. One pole, the bigger one, we dropped all the way to the bottom and let it sit five feet above the sea floor. The other line, we would drop to the bottom, reel it twice and yank it, reel it twice and yank it. We probably caught seventy or eighty fish; sometimes, you'd have four or five fish flopping on the deck, and Marquis warned us to put our shoes on to protect our feet. Once, I threw up with a fish on my line and had to hand my rod to Will so he could haul it in. I lay down on the deck, across the bow.

"Nick, get up and fish, bitch," Marquis said. "Don't be a pussy!"

I was too sick to respond.

Later I sat on the captain's bench, shaded by the canopy. It started to get windy, and I put my sweatshirt on, then looked for my orange winter jacket. Someone had moved it from the front cooler; it sat in a puddle of water, so I tried to dry it out by draping it over the cooler. I kept trying to eat because I was really hungry and thought that getting food in my stomach might help my headache. I munched on some peanuts and a sandwich, but I couldn't hold anything down, not even water.

"You look like shit," Corey said.

About four o'clock I put my jacket on, even though it was still damp. Already I had on sweatpants, gloves, a skullcap, my Nike Shoxx, everything I had brought. The chop had turned to seven-foot swells. I felt dry but very sick. We were beaten up, ready to call it a day, and started groaning about how long it would take to get back to shore. It had taken four hours, with stops, to reach the site. Now the seas were bigger. At four fifteen, Marquis told Will, "Reel your line in, that's the last fish. It's getting bad. We should head in. It's gonna take a long time to get back."

*   *   *

MARQUIS WAS DRIVING. I was sitting next to him on the captain's bench. We were probably a hundred yards downwind from the spot where the anchor sat. Marquis maneuvered the boat over the anchor, and Will began to pull up on the line. The anchor didn't budge, though. It stayed put on the bottom. Corey went to the bow and began to help. But even a 265-pound defensive end could not budge the anchor. Marquis shifted the boat to various positions for a half hour, circling the anchor as Will and Corey pulled the line from one direction, then another. They kept yanking, two big, strong, fit men, but the anchor remained stuck.

Marquis grew frustrated. The same thing had happened on our trip the week before—we couldn't raise the anchor. Finally, a friend of Marquis's who was fishing with us decided to cut the line. Then Marquis spent two hundred bucks buying a new anchor and rope. Now he was pissed.

"I'm not losing another fucking anchor," he said.

I sat with my head down, feeling awful, in no condition to help anybody. Will had an idea. We could tie the line to the back of the boat, gun the motor, and try to yank the anchor out that way. No one else had a better suggestion, so Will undid the one-inch line from the bow and tied it to a cleat on the stern. The anchor would come loose or the line would snap, Will told Marquis. If worse came to worst, we could drag whatever snagged the anchor until it came free.

Who knows what it was caught on: the shipwreck, a cable, some sort of debris. It could have been anything. There was no way to tell. Maybe it was stuck in the muck 150 feet along the bottom.

It wasn't like anyone had been pounding beers all day—not in this weather. Corey didn't drink. I had a beer and a half but had puked it all up. Will had had seven or eight; Marquis, five or six, in a period of ten hours. Everyone seemed pretty clearheaded.

"Might as well try," Marquis said of Will's idea.

As the boat rocked, Corey stood just behind me at the center console, in a wide stance, holding on to the canopy. Will stood at the back, where he had tied the anchor line. Marquis pulled the line tight and gunned the motor. It made this high-pitched sound, like a motorcycle taking off, and then a low rumbling sound, like the engine had flooded or stalled.

"Whoa!" Will said two or three times to Marquis, cautioning him not to push too hard on the throttle. He didn't get to say it again.

The blades of the anchor must have dug in more instead of coming loose. The stern squatted down, and water began to pour in; the bow raised toward the sky, and the boat began to list toward the port side.

"Get to the top!" Marquis yelled. We tried to run to the starboard side but it was too late. It all happened so quickly. There was no chance to make a Mayday call on the radio. I was sitting on the captain's bench, and I took one step and grabbed the hand railing on the starboard side of the boat. As it rolled upward, I catapulted myself into the water.

All I saw was open sea just before I went under. It was so cold. I was a little afraid, but I also felt the urge to laugh. For a moment, it seemed funny, the same feeling I used to get when I fell off a Jet Ski. Like "Oh shit!" and you kind of laugh and swim to it and flip it over and get back on. But this wasn't a Jet Ski. It was a 3,400-pound boat, more than a ton and a half. The last time I had flipped a Jet Ski, I was in high school, riding near the shoreline of Lake Erie. I wasn't in seven-foot swells in the Gulf of Mexico.

I had finally gotten dry on the boat, and now I was in the water—and it was so cold it was shocking. I was weak and tired, having thrown up my breakfast and everything else I had eaten and drunk, but my endorphins kicked in. Now I didn't seem so nauseous anymore. I was wide awake, frightened, and very alert.

We all came up to the surface at the left of the boat, within a few feet of one another. No one had a life jacket on. Our first reaction was to swim to the boat, which was completely upside down, the white hull and the propeller sticking out of the water. Hundreds—thousands—of bubbles were coming up to the surface with the release of air from below. It was like someone had dropped a giant Alka-Seltzer into the Gulf.

Corey moved toward the back of the boat and said, "We gotta flip this right away. We gotta flip it."

Marquis said, "Oh my God, oh my God." He spoke in a very serious, afraid voice. I saw the look on his face. I had never seen any of these three guys frightened before. That initial light, humorous feeling I had when I went into the water was gone. I could see that Marquis was scared. And I got scared, too.

We knew we had to try to flip the boat right away. We were afraid it would lose its air pocket underneath and sink. Immediately, we began working together. We were all athletes; we had relied on teamwork since we were kids. Maybe together we could get out of this mess. Corey swam back toward the motor, which had stopped running. I swam with him through the swells. Will and Marquis moved toward the front of the boat, on the left side.

We counted down, one-two-three, so that we would be working in unison, not pushing and pulling against one another. We tried to grip the little ridges along the hull and use our body weight to flip the boat. We tried to time it so maybe a wave would roll underneath and help us turn it upright, but we couldn't get any leverage.

The waves were smashing us against the boat, and it was hard to grip anything. Everything we could grab on to was now underwater. We would try to grab hold, but we would slide off the hull in slow motion. My heart was jumping out of my chest. "Are you fucking kidding me?" we kept saying.

We had started out the day to celebrate, and now we were in the water with no life jackets, trying to prevent a tragedy.

"Oh my God, oh my God!" I kept saying.

After we flailed about for about five minutes, Will noticed the anchor line was still attached to the back of the boat. "We've got to cut the line," he said. "It'll flip when we cut the anchor loose."

We thought the boat was being held down because the line was still supertight. We drifted the boat over to get a teeny bit of slack on the line, and then Will and Marquis cut the rope on the propeller, which was sticking out of the water. Floating at the stern, they grabbed the rope and shaved it back and forth like they were cutting wood with a saw.

It took them five minutes. Once the line was cut, the back end of the boat came up a little bit. We started drifting immediately, but my first reaction was, We're gonna be able to flip this boat now that it's not tied down. It'll be fine.

It wasn't fine. It was déjà vu from a few minutes earlier. Corey and I basically lay across the stern, kicking down with our feet and trying to yank the boat toward us with our arms, hoping a wave would roll underneath and help us flip it. Marquis and Will tried to yank the boat from near the front, then they got in the water and tried to push upward from the starboard side. There was no way. Physics made it impossible. No one could get any leverage. The more Will and Marquis pushed upward, the deeper they plunged underwater. And the center console was now below the surface acting as a giant, resistant rudder. It wasn't like we barely missed flipping the boat over or like we might have done it with a little more strength or one more guy. As strong as all of us were—and together we could bench press a ton and shove aside or block or tackle even the biggest human impediment on the football field—that boat didn't come within 5 percent of flipping back over.

"I can't believe we can't fucking flip this thing," Corey said.

Will kept trying to think of things. Nothing worked.

"I'm so sorry, you guys," Marquis said after about a half hour in the water. He must have said it ten times. I think he felt it was his fault because he was the captain. He was in charge. He held the responsibility. This was his boat, and he thought he would lose it and lose us and himself, too.

"I can't believe this," he said. "I'm so sorry."

"Dude, don't worry," we told Marquis. "It's not your fault. We'll get out of it."

Not long before we flipped, we had seen a giant cargo vessel hauling shipping containers. You could make out the colors of the containers, but the ship wasn't close. It was in the distance and it definitely hadn't seen us. Or if it had, it had given no indication. Besides, it could not have predicted what was about to happen.

"Where the fuck did that boat go?" we asked a bunch of times. But it was long gone.

There were nearly two hours of sunlight left when we first turned over. But the day began to exhaust itself. By now, it was about five thirty. Sunset was approaching in an hour. The water got rougher. It seemed louder now, too, random waves crashing against our backs, pushing us underwater as we tried to hold on to the boat. Will spoke up: "We're gonna lose sunlight. We gotta start thinking about tonight."

It was clear now we wouldn't be rescued before dark. Will began to take charge. He asked Marquis if he had an emergency beacon that could transmit our position. The answer was no. Will kept asking questions: Did Marquis have any flares aboard? Did he have a CB radio that would work? Could we get to the drinking water? Where were the life jackets located?

"We need as many supplies as we can get," Will said.

We had been in the water about forty-five minutes. We had wind jackets, wind pants, sweatpants, and jackets, but they were soaked through. Already, we were all shivering. I think everyone was starting to think to themselves, This is real. Oh my God. There's a good chance we might not make it out of this.

Will kept asking questions, but we were all scared, cold, and in shock. It took awhile for Marquis to answer. Water flew into his mouth, and he would have to spit it out before he could speak. He told Will that the life jackets were in the storage closet at the center console, now above the steering wheel on the overturned boat. I remembered seeing something orange when I put my backpack in there; I figured they were life jackets, but I hadn't thought much about it.

"Okay, I'll try to get them," Will said.

The bin sat at an angle, three or four feet wide and high. There was other stuff inside, like my book bag, a case of beer, chips and pretzels, the bumpers that Marquis used when he docked the boat. Without life jackets, there was no way we would make it through the night. Not in this water, in this cold, in these crashing waves. Will edged toward the center of the boat and went under. He came up quickly the first time.

"I can't see anything," he said.

He took off his green wind jacket and wind pants, thinking this would make him less buoyant so he could more easily get under the boat. He had lost his flip-flops when we fell into the water. All he was wearing now was a tan or gray T-shirt and his swim trunks.

Marquis took off his T-shirt, wind jacket, and wind pants, stripping down to his swim trunks. He let his clothes go—they weren't a priority at the moment. He went under for about two seconds and came back up. He didn't say anything. He went under again. This time he came back in about three seconds. Again, he didn't say a word. He tried a third time and resurfaced after about five seconds.

"I can't get under," Marquis said.

Will looked at me and asked, "Nick, will you try? Can you get under there?"

I was scared shitless. Will was one of the best swimmers I knew. Marquis was a ridiculous athlete. I had just watched them fail at trying to get under the boat. Corey was saying, "Oh my God, I can't believe this!" It freaked me out.

Not that I couldn't get under there. I was just scared to try. Scared for my life. I had never done that before, never opened my eyes in salt water. I was sick. We had no life jackets. I was freezing and petrified.

"No, I can't," I told Will, kind of stuttering. I was embarrassed. It was one of the first times I ever said no without having tried something.

Will rolled his eyes at me.

He was determined to get the life jackets. He was a take-charge guy. When he was in the sixth or seventh grade and his mother didn't want him to play football, he filled out the forms anyway and told his parents, "You need to sign; I'm playing." When he was fourteen or so, he and his father pushed away from their dock one day, and the boat wouldn't start. Finally, they got the engine going, and his father asked Will what he would have done if they had remained stranded, just drifting off the dock.

"Dad, don't worry about it," he said. "I would have thought of something."

Now Will was in another situation, much more dangerous, but he was firm in his insistence to retrieve the life jackets.

"I think I can get to that closet," he said. He was getting loud and frustrated. "Okay," he asked Marquis again, "are they in that closet?"

Will must have dived under six or seven times. He and Marquis would go back and forth. Marquis would explain where everything was. Finally, Will went under the boat and came up with two life jackets, the standard bright orange kind that slip around your neck and clasp in the front. He submerged again and found a third life jacket. Then he spotted a seat cushion that must have come from a bin beneath one of the two chairs at the stern of the boat. Marquis, Corey, and I slipped the life jackets on. Will slipped his arms through two straps on the cushion and put it on his back like a turtle's shell. "Thanks," we told Will. I felt bad that he and Marquis were doing all the work, but there wasn't much that Corey and I could do.

Will had also ripped loose the twenty-gallon cooler that sat in front of the center console. It popped to the surface. Everything had come loose inside and sunk or got stuck under the boat. Only a gallon jug of water was in there. It kind of fell out and floated away. We let it go—didn't think anything of it.

We grabbed the cooler, though. If the boat sank, we would be desperate to grab on to something that could float. Without any discussion about who would go where, we climbed into unsteady positions on the upside-down boat, all of us facing the bow.

Everything was inverted. The propeller stuck out of the water. To the right of the motor was a tiny ladder attached to a swim platform, which stuck out from the stern like a lunchroom tray. On either side of the motor at the stern, trim tabs jutted out about a foot and a half or two feet. On an upright boat, the swim platform provided a place to sit or put on a pair of skis or launch a dip into the water. The platform and the ladder also helped swimmers board the boat. Trim tabs were controllable stainless-steel plates that helped adjust the pitch attitude of a boat—the degree to which the bow tilted up or down. The tabs helped a boat get on plane quickly, reduced pounding, and corrected listing to port or starboard. Now the ladder, swim platform, and trim tabs all had another unintended usage: life-saving equipment.

I stood to the right of the motor, out of the water from about midthigh, holding the outboard with my left hand. I had my left foot on the swim platform or just below, on a trim tab.

Will stood near me. We were in a tight space, and he kept stepping on my foot. He kind of straddled the motor in the water, his left leg perched somehow on the outboard or just dangling. Corey stood on a trim tab to the left of the motor. Marquis basically got on his hands and knees on the hull, his chest pressing on the cooler. He braced his feet against the motor, held the cooler with his left hand and reached with his right hand to grab my right ankle once I propped my foot on the hull. There was nothing else to grab on to.

"We gotta hold on to this cooler," we kept saying.

We had to shout to hear one another. Someone would say something, and another guy would ask, "Huh? What?" It was loud from the wind and the waves crashing and slamming us into the boat—it was a constant barrage. A wave would crash into us, and someone would start coughing from taking in salt water. Every surface was slick and hard to grip. Marquis, exposed to the chilly air atop the hull, wore only a life jacket and his bathing suit. I had on my sweatshirt, orange jacket, sweatpants, skull cap, and gloves. Corey was still wearing his black wind jacket and wind pants. Will was down to his T-shirt and trunks. Corey had held on to his wind gear while Will went under the boat, but later we lost the jacket and pants. They must have gotten swept away.

Near sunset, it went from being small swells and quick waves to waves coming in all different directions, whitecaps, choppy, the scariest thing. We couldn't figure out the current or the rhythm of the waves. The wind sounded like a constant whistle in the air, *ffffffff*, like someone holding a compressor or a tire deflating. We were able to stay on the boat by working together. It was overcast, so we never saw a real sunset, just a gradual loss of light. The temperature felt like it was dropping dramatically. It seemed like the cold front Marquis had told us about was coming through.

Around seven o'clock, Corey said a couple times, "I ain't going out like this." Around that time, something seemed to occur to him. "What about the cell phones?" he wondered.

Will asked where they were.

There was still some dim light, so we could still see enough for one trip under the boat.

Marquis told Will about his and Corey's cell phones. They were stored in a Ziploc bag, along with their keys and Marquis's camera. The bag was stored in a bin in the boat's inverted canopy. Will swam back under the boat and found the bag. He also brought up a couple of flares. Eventually, we stuck the flares in Marquis's swimsuit so they wouldn't float away. My right hand was free, and I had the most stable position on the boat, so they gave me the bag.

Corey had an iPhone, which I didn't know how to use, so I grabbed Marquis's phone. I think it was a BlackBerry. It was dry and turned on immediately. There was a sigh of relief. At least until I dialed 9-1-1 with my free hand. As we rocked back and forth and every which way, the phone just kept saying CALLING . . . CALLING . . . CALLING. There was no connection. Someone said there were probably no cell phone towers within range. There were no reception bars on the phone, but I thought this wasn't supposed to matter when you dialed an emergency number.

"I thought 9-1-1 was supposed to work anywhere," I told the others in frustration. "Shouldn't a satellite pick it up?"

Then I went to Marquis's call log. I held the motor with my left hand and held the phone in my right hand, dialing with my right thumb. I called Marquis's wife, Rebekah. No signal, it said. I tried my girlfriend Paula. Same thing. We were well out of cell phone range. They were supposed to work up to twenty or thirty miles out, but on our trip the week before, Marquis had lost phone contact before we even lost sight of land.

I tried 9-1-1 again. Nothing. Every time I tried to call someone on Marquis's log, it instantly said NO SERVICE. When I tried to text, I kept getting NO SERVICE . . . SEND WHEN SERVICE AVAILABLE? I kept pressing YES, hoping that if we drifted into range, it would send, even if the phone wasn't on.

At first, I left Corey's off to preserve the power so I could use it later, and tried Marquis's phone every five or ten minutes. Nothing. Always nothing.

"Anything?" Will would ask. "Anything?"

It was more of a reflex than a hope. They knew if I got anything, I'd scream it out.

"I can't believe this shit," Corey said.

Will kept thinking back to his idea to tie the anchor line to the back of the boat.

"I'm so stupid," he would say. "I can't believe I did that."

"It's not your fault," I told him. "No one had a better idea."

WE BEGAN TO wonder when someone would notice that we had not returned. We had not given a precise time about coming back, only a general idea. "What time will Rebekah realize something's wrong?" we asked Marquis. "When is she gonna call to report us overdue?"

Marquis said he usually called her when the boat was about five miles out from shore. Last weekend, he had called her at eight thirty or nine. He told her he would be home earlier this time. Still, he wasn't sure at what point she would become alarmed.

"There's times I told her we would be earlier and then we have good fishing and I'm later," Marquis said while kneeling on the hull. But he added, "There's no way she wouldn't call the Coast Guard by two o'clock."

We figured it would be much later than that before someone came looking for us.

I HAVE A fear of sharks, and around eight o'clock I asked, "Is there any chance sharks could get us right now?"

"No, don't worry, they're too stupid," Will said.

Marquis also said not to worry about it. "They'd be afraid of that big white boat," he said. "They think it's another animal."

Their reassurances calmed me. I didn't really think about it again that night. There were plenty of other things to worry about.

It was dark. My teeth were constantly chattering. All of our teeth were chattering. I was still sick, a little nauseous from earlier and from the constant bucking of the boat, but I didn't feel nearly as bad as before.

"God it's cold," Corey said.

The waves kept pounding us. Marquis was in a precarious position atop the hull, trying to secure the cooler, nothing really firm to hold on to except my leg. He slid one way, then the other. He would nearly go off one side, and we would grab him and pull him up.

I desperately kept trying to hold on to the Ziploc bag so I wouldn't lose the phones, keys, and wallets. I probably should have put the bag in my coat pocket, but it didn't occur to me. I was still in the same position, my left hand on the motor and my right hand free, like I was riding a bull. I held on to that bag as tight as I could.

"Try it again," Corey kept saying about the phone. Every time, I got the same response: NO SERVICE.

Marquis kept climbing back into position on the hull, but he looked fatigued. He was in tremendous shape, but he had almost no body fat to insulate him against the cold.

"You good?" we kept asking him.

"Yeah, I'm good," he said, but he seemed tired.

The waves seemed to get rougher after sunset. And a little louder. Consistent eight-footers now. They were capping.

The storm was coming in.

A LITTLE LATER, I said to Marquis and Corey, "All I know is, when we get out of this, you both better hook me up with damn good seats to a game next season."

"Oh yeah," Marquis promised, laughing.

"Hell yeah, boy," Corey said. "Amen to that."

Corey had a watch on, a waterproof Nike with a dial that lit up green when he pressed a button. It helped us keep track of time. Around nine o'clock, we said the Lord's Prayer:

> *Our Father, who art in Heaven, Hallowed be thy name.*
> *Thy kingdom come, Thy will be done on earth as it is in*
> *heaven.*
> *Give us this day our daily bread.*
> *And forgive us our trespasses, as we forgive those who trespass*
> *against us.*
> *And lead us not into temptation, but deliver us from evil.*
> *Amen.*

I'm not very religious. I knew the prayer from football and other sports. I didn't know all the words, but I said the ones I knew.

It was like a song where you don't know all the lyrics: you just keep singing or humming along anyway. I think we said the Our Father twice more as a group.

Corey added small prayers, "Please God, give me strength."

It seemed to be getting rougher and colder. The wind picked up, consistently blowing maybe fifteen to twenty miles an hour. Random gusts sounded like a loud roar, like a fan boat flying by. At times, your face felt dry, then all of a sudden you would be absolutely demolished by the water. I could feel my cheeks shaking, like when you're on a roller coaster. My lips were blistering from the cold and the wind.

Throughout the night, we kept looking toward the bow. I kept asking Will for confirmation, "Is the front end of the boat getting lower and lower?"

I was terrified that it would sink.

"I think it is getting lower," Will would say, but it was hard to tell. The sky was overcast. There was very little light. I could see probably halfway up the hull. Maybe not even that far.

Marquis kept getting mad at me. I was dehydrated. I couldn't even hold down any water once I got seasick. I hadn't eaten or drunk anything in hours. Now I was cramping up from lack of fluids and from keeping my leg in the same position. My right foot was still on the hull to give Marquis something to hold on to, but when my leg knotted up, I had to move my foot, adjust my position.

"What are you doing?" Marquis kept asking.

"I'm cramping up!" I'd yell. "Hold up a second!"

Later, I gave him a warning so he could brace himself.

"All right, hurry up!" he said.

He was in a precarious position, but none of us were really secure as the waves kept crashing on us in the dark. We'd hear them approach and we'd scream, "Hold on!" trying to brace ourselves. The hull was slippery; the cooler kept shifting. Marquis clung to my ankle as he flopped to the left side, then to the right, like windshield wipers. Then he fell off the boat. It was like trying to ride a bucking bronco. He must have come off the boat twenty or thirty times.

I had a somewhat more reliable position, with someplace to plant my feet. So did Corey and Will. Still, I probably came off the boat fifteen times. Sometimes you would climb halfway back up and a wave would come and throw you right back down. Sometimes you were thrown clear, and it took ten or fifteen seconds to get back to the boat, which you could barely make out in the dark. I kept holding on to that bag with the phones, making sure it was sealed and holding it as high as possible when I splashed into the water.

Then I got nailed by a wave and I went in the water with Marquis's phone out of the bag. I was trying to grab on to something and a wave caught me unaware. I held the phone and the bag, and climbed back on, but I knew this couldn't be good. The key pad stayed lit, but the screen went dark. It was dead.

"Shit, this phone's done," I said.

I put Marquis's phone in the bag and grabbed Corey's. He told me how to use the iPhone, yelling out the instructions over the wind and the water, but the glass screen was slippery, making it difficult to use the keyboard. With a regular cell phone, I could hold it in my right hand and dial with my thumb. With an iPhone I needed both hands.

I would lean into the motor to balance myself and try to make a call. I phoned Rebekah and Paula, but still nothing. Then I tried to send a mass text—"help 9-1-1" and "help, flipd bot"—to Corey's phone log. I was texting as fast as I could so I wouldn't keep the phone exposed and lose it in the water. But I kept getting the same message as before: NO SERVICE . . . SEND WHEN SERVICE AVAILABLE? I kept hitting YES, hoping against hope. I tried to dial 9-1-1, but it replied with the same disheartening message that Marquis's phone had: CONNECTING . . . CONNECTING . . . CONNECTING.

I tried holding the phone as high as I could with my right hand, hoping it would somehow catch a signal and dial through or show our coordinates, whatever. Still nothing. "I thought 9-1-1 was supposed to work anywhere!" I said again. I guess I was wrong. It didn't work in a storm seventy miles out in the Gulf.

Sometimes I would hold Corey's iPhone up and hope the light from the dial would let me see the front of the boat. It didn't. I continued to ask Will if it was getting lower. I must have asked him a dozen times. It was a constant fight now, the boat rocking, trying to hold on and protect the phone. If you let yourself relax for more than ten or fifteen seconds, you would be in the water.

If we hadn't worked so well together, getting the life jackets from under the boat, holding on to Marquis on the hull, helping one another back onto the stern and hull when we fell in, chances are one of us would have been swept away real quick.

Once, between waves, Corey said again in a determined voice, "There ain't no way I'm going out like this!"

But a grim resignation was starting to set in as we clung to the boat and the Gulf battered us. There were a lot of "Oh my Gods." At first it was, "Oh my God, is this really happening?" Now it was, "Oh my God, is this it?"

About midnight, Corey interrupted our silence, shouting, "I can't believe the four of us can't flip this boat!" He seemed angry and discouraged. Then he said, "There's gotta be a way. What haven't we tried? We gotta try again."

Will and I reminded him, "Dude, there's no leverage. It's not possible."

Maybe if it were a ten-foot boat in five-foot seas it would have been possible. Not out here.

"Think how hard it was just to get the cooler out of the water," Will said. It had taken two of us just to get the water out and flip it onto the boat.

It got quiet. We were all freezing and exhausted. We began to huddle together, cuddling almost, trying to stay warm as the night went on. From the stern, I leaned forward until my ear and cheek were on Marquis's back as he rested on the hull. Will also leaned forward, placing his chest on my back. Corey, too, leaned in from the stern, our three heads gathering in front of the motor, on Marquis's torso. I thought for a moment that it was weird, four grown men clustered together like puppies or kittens, but it was necessary if we were going to maintain any body heat. I could feel everybody shivering and hear their teeth chattering.

Once, when it was quiet, knowing how desperate our situation was, I said, "I love you guys." I just wanted to let them know how I felt. No one said anything back. It was a little awkward, but I knew from their reactions that everyone was thinking the same thing.

Bunched up there like that, we talked sporadically, sometimes about our families, sometimes about the things we would do different with our lives. Different paths we might have chosen. In the middle of the Gulf, with our boat overturned and the four of us getting tossed about by waves in a storm, our priorities seemed to straighten. Little crap didn't matter. Being stranded, facing the possibility that we would all die, left us almost with a guilty feeling about things we had left undone. Marquis and Corey talked about their hometowns, their parents, college football, playing in the NFL. Marquis, of course, mentioned his love for Rebekah and Goose. Corey, who wasn't married, reflected on his mother and what she meant to him. At one point, he said, "The things I would change." He didn't say anything specific, but there was regret in his voice.

Will said he wished he had been closer to his older brother, Blake. I had never met him. Will was single, a ladies' man, an athlete. Blake had a steady girlfriend and would be married in eight months. Will lived in Tampa and had worked in finance until the economy went bad and his firm closed its office. Lately he had been splitting his time between Tampa and Crystal River, his hometown, where he and Blake helped out their parents at the family tire and auto shop that they had run for three decades. I think Will wished he had given a little more effort with his brother.

I thought about my mom, Marcia, and how much I loved her and how upset she got when something happened to me or my sister, Kristen. She always put herself second—or third or fourth—so that

Kristen and I could have a good life. My parents had had a rough marriage. The details are private, no one's business but their own. My mom stuck it out until I had just about finished my senior year of high school. They would argue and she would always try to be the peacemaker. "Don't worry, I'm fine," she would always tell us. I know it was hard on her, but she always seemed more concerned about how we were doing.

After I graduated, she took us on a vacation to Cancun. She was always doing something for me. When I was in elementary school in Ohio, she volunteered, helping take attendance, selling magazines for fund-raisers, chaperoning us on field trips. At night, I would lay on her lap to watch TV and when she told me to go to bed, I'd say, "No, I'm just going to rest my eyes."

Nick Butt, she called me.

In high school, she never missed one of my games. She kept stats and a scrapbook of newspaper clippings about my basketball and football careers. After she and my father split, she worked as a paralegal and took out loans so that I could attend Kent State my freshman and sophomore years. When I moved to Florida in 2005, and worked painting jobs for my dad's business, my mother put her foot down and said she couldn't help support me; she told me to go back to school, that it was the right thing to do. When I applied to USF and was too nervous to call the admissions office, she called for me to find out whether I had been accepted. While I was in school, she let me charge food on her credit card.

Eventually, she moved to Florida to be near my sister and me. I played flag football on Saturday mornings, and she drove up two hours from Fort Myers to Tampa to watch my games. Sometimes she cooked or cleaned my house. She bought the orange jacket I was wearing out here in the cold water.

My dad, Stu, busted his ass with his painting business when we were all in Ohio. When I was a kid, we had a vacation home in Orlando. Every Christmas break, we'd hook up our thirty-foot camper and drive to Disney World. On other holidays, we would go to Myrtle Beach or Virginia Beach. In the winter, we skied in Vermont, in Killington. I got anything I wanted. I was spoiled. Four-wheelers, Jet Skis.

Being in the water made me think about an accident that happened in my junior year of high school. I was sixteen, and I begged and begged to get a motorcycle. Let's go look, my dad said. I ended up getting a Suzuki GSX-R600. A crotch rocket. My best friend and I went to watch a football game and had some people over to my house afterward. During the party, I took him out real quick through a dark neighborhood around a bass lake. We weren't drinking, but we were speeding. The street looked like a straightaway, but it happened to have a turn. We went down. I must have skidded thirty yards, bouncing on my hands across the pavement. I was bruised and scratched up but I didn't hit my head or get badly hurt. I ran over to my friend, Daniel Turner. I didn't have a phone on me. I began screaming for help. He was unconscious, bleeding from both ears. When the ambulance showed up, Dan had awakened and was freaking out. He was swearing and throwing punches at the emergency people. He had a concussion and they put him in a neck brace. If he hadn't been wearing a helmet, he would have died.

He had two emergency brain surgeries to relieve the pressure and the swelling. When we got to the hospital, I knew his parents were there, and I didn't know if he would live or die. Up to this point, it was the most scared I'd ever been in my life. I didn't know if his dad was going to hug me or attack me. Dan was in the hospital more than a month doing rehab. As scared as I was then, though, being stranded in the Gulf now was a lot worse. It was kind of like it was in God's hands. At least then, there was help to be found. Out here there was nothing. Whoever came to look for us would be looking for a needle in a haystack.

I knew my dad would worry about me. He had moved to Florida, to Tarpon Springs. He still had his painting business, but he had been through some hard times—divorce, financial issues. I thought about that. I thought, If I don't get out of this, it's going to make his life that much harder. I knew he was proud of me. I knew both of my parents were proud of me. They thought I always did what I wanted, whether it was good or bad. I think they respected me for that. They knew once I made my mind up about something, the only person who could keep me from doing it was myself, whether it was me not doing my homework or trying to make the USF football team.

My mom used to say to me when I was younger, "Nick if you apply yourself in school, you'll do well. You are smart, if you'd just apply yourself." I didn't like school. I applied myself to sports and having a good time. I didn't like school at all. I hated school. I got a communications degree from USF in 2008, but I thought it was just one step above "undecided." I just went because my mom wanted me to and I knew it was expected. I had a diploma, but I didn't have a plan to use my degree. At the same time, being a personal trainer was something I worked hard at and loved and made a decent living at.

My sister used to tell me I got the looks, she got the brains—not that she's bad-looking. Kristen was twenty-seven, three years older than me. We've always been pretty close. She was an athlete. She is tall, 5 feet 9 inches, with light brown hair and a strong, athletic build. She played shortstop and the outfield in fast-pitch softball in high school. Once, she played in a tournament in Lyon, France. She had scholarship offers to places like Ohio State, but she wanted to go to school in Florida, at USF. When I was younger, I wanted to be like her. She was my idol. She was cool and popular and hung out with the jocks. She could always kick my ass. She'd hold me down and threaten to spit in my face. My parents spoiled her in ways different from me. She had a car and big parties, a hundred-plus people. When she went to school at USF, they had a house built for her in Tampa.

We differed in a big way as far as schooling went. She looked forward to school and liked it. It came natural to her. She was always studying. In high school, she was already taking courses at community college. She graduated from college at twenty. She went back to Ohio and finished her undergraduate degree at Kent State. She always had a job, even when she didn't necessarily need one. Then she got her MBA at Cleveland State when she was twenty-three.

Now she worked as a rep for a company that distributed dental supplies. She and my mom were living together in Fort Myers. Kristen is so driven. That's what I love about her. I always used to say, "It sucks, here I am, twenty-three and I just finished college, and my sister had her master's when she was twenty-three."

The other important woman in my life, Paula Oliveira, was nonstop in the back of my head all night. I knew she would be worried. When I left in the morning, I popped my head in the bedroom and said, "Babe, I gotta go. Love you." She said, "No, I need a kiss," so I walked in and kissed her.

Paula was five years older, a dance teacher at a performing arts middle school and at a studio in Tampa. She is a brunette, in as good a shape as I was in. Strong as hell. Her family was from Sao Paulo, Brazil. When I moved to Tampa in 2005, I only knew a few people in town. Paula was already out of school, in her first year of teaching, and I met her about six months after I got to town. She went to USF—she and my sister actually lived for a brief time in the same dorm; and while they weren't friends, they had mutual friends. I met her while a group of us were out for drinks. After that night, I kept calling Paula and texting, but she gave me the run-around. I was twenty, she was twenty-four or twenty-five. I couldn't even drink in a bar yet. Not legally. Her friends would tell me, "She thinks you're too young."

About a month later—this would have been November 2005—we started hanging out. One night we went out and she said she realized that she liked me. She likes to say that it was the happiest night of my life. When we first started dating, I was working out to try to make the USF football team. I had all these motivational quotes in my bedroom, all around my computer: Push yourself to the limit. Shut up and train. Squat 'til you puke. On my twenty-first birthday, she bought me an ice-cream cake. Most people turn twenty-one, they go out and drink twenty-one shots. I was training hard, on a strict diet. I had dedicated myself to the diet and to making the team.

When I saw what she had brought me, I felt bad. "Thank you so much," I told her, "but I can't eat that cake."

"Are you serious?" she said.

I trained her for a while in the gym, and there were times when she felt she couldn't lift a pound, and I'd say, "Bullshit, you know you have it," and she could always do two or three more reps. I made her nervous at first when I worked out. I was so intense, I would be bench-pressing and when she thought I couldn't lift any more, I'd yell, "light weight, light weight," and I'd lift it up. I think she was afraid I would drop the weight on my neck. But if she thought I was crazy, I guess she thought it was a good crazy.

She reminded me of my mom. Paula would always go the extra mile to make you happy and take care of you and make the little things bigger, whether it was breakfast in bed or cleaning the house. "Don't do that," she would say. "Don't worry about cleaning the dishes. I'll do it." No bickering or fighting.

We had three dogs, and I wondered if they would miss me. Chloe was Paula's, a boxer, four years old, fifty-three pounds. A momma's girl, a big baby. The other two were Jack Russells. Kelli, twelve, was Miss Independent, smart, always bringing home frogs and lizards, a bird, a snake. She got a rabbit once, too. Tori, nine, was a wild child. She ran the house, nipping at everyone's ankles. She'd bite you one minute and lick you the next. I thought she was bipolar. When visitors came, she went under the stairs outside and dug a hole. I had no idea why. At night, we all had our spots on the bed. Chloe was at the foot. Tori was usually between Paula's legs or against her. Kelli would get between us or on my left side. Would they notice that I was gone? Could they sense that something was wrong?

For a long period that first night, there wasn't much else to do but try to stay on the boat and think. I wished I hadn't been so selfish, hurting girls' feelings, being mean to family members over stupid things. I remembered my first Thanksgiving in Tampa, in 2005. I had spent it alone. My roommates were gone. I remember being sad and upset. If I got out of this, I would never let myself feel that way again—distant and selfish.

I thought about football. How I should have played my final two years in high school. What's two years now? How I should have sat out the 2006 season at USF and played in 2007. I kept thinking about getting rescued and making it to those games to see Marquis and Corey play. I kept thinking about what a good story this was going to be to tell once we got out of this. And then, at times, I thought there was no way in hell we were going to get out of it.

I don't know if it was the trainer in me or what, but about every half hour I would remind the guys, "Make sure you move your toes a lot, move your feet, flex your chest, shrug your shoulders, get your blood flowing." I think they did—at first, anyway.

As the night went on, Will, Corey, and I did the most of the talking. Marquis seemed to get quieter and quieter.

"Coop, you good?" we would ask. "You all right?"

"I'm all right," he would say.

Then we didn't hear from him for a while. Marquis had been on the hull on his hands and knees, holding on to the cooler in case the boat sank, wearing only his swim trunks and his life jacket. With the boat bucking and rolling, he had fallen off so many times, he seemed exhausted.

"Coop?" we called out. "Coop?"

His responses became slower and slower. At first, he would answer right when we called his name. Now we'd call out four or five times before he said anything. Sometimes we had to shake him on the hull.

He started to slur and ramble a little. Maybe it was around two thirty. The water was still rough, crashing in. Marquis had taken in so much salt water and had done a lot of gagging. Then he began to dry heave. His teeth were chattering constantly.

Once, we got wiped out bad, constantly, for about twenty minutes straight, every one of us. Giant waves, all at once. It was scary as hell, the boat heaving up and down, the whitecaps pounding us and flinging everyone away from the boat, all of us scrambling desperately to get back within reach.

For a few moments, I could only see Will. Marquis and Corey had disappeared, and I started freaking out until I spotted them again. I was knocked a good ten feet from the boat a couple times in a row. I started screaming out.

What light there was seemed to come from the whiteness of the hull. When you were at the stern, or in the water facing the boat, you could see the hull and the outline of people's bodies. Sometimes, if they were close enough, you could see their eyes and teeth and maybe their life jackets. But if you faced away from the boat, into the black, you could hardly see your hand in front of your face. Sometimes when you went in the water and got disoriented, you just had to swim toward peoples' voices.

WILL REACHED AND grabbed me and pulled me to the boat. Then Will lost his grip, and I grabbed him; and then we both grabbed Corey. Marquis kept falling off, and we grabbed his leg or his arm. It was all adrenaline—there was no time to think.

Marquis was getting into bad shape. He would take longer and longer to respond—and when he did, he was mumbling. He slid off the hull to the back of the boat, to the left of the motor, near Corey. Then he started trying to move around the left side of the boat, trying to go somewhere, trying to get something. "What are you doing?" I asked him.

I don't know if he thought, I've got to do something now, or what. It wasn't him, not the Marquis I knew. He was an incredibly fit athlete, but I guess hypothermia was taking control of him. He was mumbling, "I need to get the anchor. I've got to get under the boat."

Marquis got away a couple times, and Corey grabbed his life jacket to keep him from going under. He was very wild with his arms, his head lolling. He looked like a person who had been drinking for days—very incoherent, his eyes every which way, randomly dry-heaving. His mouth was kind of foaming. I was only a foot or two from him. He would turn around, and when I saw his face, I knew it wasn't him.

As Marquis deteriorated, we lost the cooler. We had it on the hull, and then it slipped and filled with water. "Do we need this cooler?" I asked. It was rough and hard to hold on to. Will said, "No, let it go."

Would the cooler help us if we lost the boat? Maybe, but it was too much work to keep it. It disappeared into the waves.

Whenever I could, I called 9-1-1 on Corey's iPhone. Still the same as before. CONNECTING . . . CONNECTING . . . CONNECTING. . . . It would just go on forever: dot, dot, dot. Then I got wiped out again and lost the Ziploc bag with Marquis's and Corey's phones inside. Now we had no way to try to communicate with our families or rescuers. But we had a bigger concern.

I kept checking the front of the boat.

"Still up," Will would say. I don't know if this was wishful thinking or what. Neither of us could see all the way to the front, just the highest point of the hull.

We weren't entirely confident. It seemed like it was getting a little lower in the water as the night went on.

"Please stay up, please stay up," we said. But I kept thinking about shipwrecks, and I wondered, "Why would this boat stay up?"

Will and I started saying, "Let's talk about this. We've got to start preparing for what happens if the boat goes under."

Corey got pissed. "What the hell are you talking about?" he said in a fierce voice, yelling above the hammering of the waves. "Once that boat goes under, we're gone!"

We kept talking. We had to have a plan. I said to Will: "No matter what, we need to stay on our backs, float with our heads in the air, and hold on to one another's life jackets."

We didn't have any other options, really. In these stormy waters, we could only cling to the boat like fleas on a rabid dog.

I thought to myself that Corey was right. If this boat goes under, we're done.

Marquis was still, and mostly silent, in the water at the back of the boat, near Corey. Then he got this rowdy energy and started trying again to go where his feverish mind was telling him—under the boat to cut the anchor. I had climbed onto the hull now and held on to Marquis's life jacket as he tried to pull away.

Corey grabbed his jacket, too.

"Don't let go of that jacket," I screamed at Corey. "Don't let him get away."

Corey yelled, "Coop, what are you doing?"

We tried to explain to him: We cut the anchor already. We cut the rope. I had thrown my leg over the outboard and straddled it. I was facing away from the bow now, the propeller jutting up near my face. We struggled with Marquis, me pulling him and Corey pushing, and finally we hoisted him out of the water and into my lap. I put my feet under a trim tab or the swim platform. That way I could brace myself while I held Marquis.

He kept fighting and fighting, slurring his words, making random sounds. He would gag and cough and dry-heave. I didn't know what to do. I tried to hold him, but he was using his strength against me. I had to use every muscle in my body, from my toes to my back to my arms, to keep him under control.

I knew this wasn't Marquis. *Uhhhh, ohhhh,* was all he could manage to say. We were yelling, "Get it together, Coop. Come on. You're gonna see Rebekah soon. You'll see Delaney soon."

I was straddling the motor and he was laying perpendicular to me, his head under my left armpit, his lower back under my right arm. I bear-hugged him, clamping on him like the shoulder restraints on a roller coaster. We were stomach to stomach, almost navel to navel. The harder he fought to do whatever he thought he had to do, the harder I squeezed down on him. He would calm down for a time. Then a bad wave would hit and slam his back against the motor, and that would set him off again.

This seemed to go on for an hour. By now it was clear that Marquis was hallucinating. He must have said it twenty times: "I've got to get under the boat, got to get the anchor, got to cut the line." He wriggled and struggled against my grip, trying to get away. If he fell off the boat, all of us grabbed him and flipped him back on.

Marquis also kept trying to take off his life jacket. It was hiked up tight around his neck from the way I was pushing against him. It must have felt like it was choking him. He would get it halfway off, and we would pull it back on and make it tighter.

Will was at the back of the boat, to the right of the motor, holding on to it with his left hand while holding on to Marquis's life jacket with his right. Marquis continued to let out a random moan every couple of minutes, five seconds at a time, low pitch to high. He would fight for ten or fifteen seconds and then lay there. The more he fought, the more I clamped down. At times he would wriggle away for a few seconds. He was strong as hell. I slapped him across the face a half dozen times, saying "Coop, Coop—get it together!" trying to wake him up, trying to make him aware.

Will and I kept working together. We noticed that Corey had begun to slump a little, too. He was wearing his black wind jacket and wind pants, but he was sinking lower off the back of the boat, down and down until he was in the water up to his chest. Earlier, he had been out of the water, standing on a trim tab. Now he was sinking, still holding on to the back of the boat, but floundering, getting quieter, shivering. He would mutter, and then he would let out a loud, random scream. I jumped a couple of times.

Earlier, Corey was more vocal and impatient with Marquis. At one point he yelled, "Come on, Coop, why are you doing this?"

"It's not him," I said. "Stop."

Corey thought Marquis had lost it mentally, but it was so far past that. I was beginning to think he was in God's hands.

I had short white socks and sneakers on, but my feet were hurting so bad, a sharp, sharp pain. I had kept doing my little calisthenics, trying to move my arms and legs to keep the blood flowing, but now my feet were killing me. My big toes were flexed upward, straining under the trim tab or the swim platform, trying to balance myself while I clutched Marquis in my lap. They were frozen numb.

Oh my God, I've got frostbite, I kept telling myself.

I've had numb feet from icing my ankles in football and basketball, but this was much worse. Because my big toes were pointed up and all the blood was in one spot, and they were so cold. It was a mixture of a dead numbness and sharp pain. I could barely move them. I kept thinking, If I get out of this, I'm going to lose my frickin' toes or both my feet.

A couple times, Marquis came off the boat. It just couldn't be helped. A wave would crash on the bow, but since I was facing the other way I couldn't see it coming, and I would smash my balls against the motor. Everything was tender in the salt water. My skin was pruny. I could feel that my legs were cut up, tender and sore.

So many times we screamed out in pain as we were bashed against the boat or slammed up against the motor. Will cut his hands. I had on cotton gloves—they were too small; I think they were my mother's—and the fingers were starting to rip. I gashed my hand on the propeller.

As I held Marquis, I kept my right leg up in the air a little higher so I could press his legs closer to my body. I was holding 215 pounds, and my shoulders, lower abs, groin, and hip flexor were on fire. It felt like I had a hernia; my leg felt locked and useless.

I kept telling Will, "You gotta help me, he's frickin' strong. I don't know how long I can do this."

It was one of the worst workouts I had been through times a hundred. We had been awake for twenty-four hours and in the water for almost twelve hours. It was like we had gone through a twelve-hour workout without anything to eat or drink, just non-stop. There weren't two minutes to relax. Will and I were working together, our conversations shorter, most all of them focused on Marquis.

After an hour of fighting for ten or fifteen or twenty seconds at a time, Marquis began to slow down. It was close to five o'clock in the morning. Now the struggle would be short, one short strain, a moan, and that was it. He wasn't trying to move or wriggle so hard anymore. I was able to save some energy. And holding him so close, I became warmer—or at least I didn't get any colder. I was sitting mostly out of the water, and my winter jacket, sweatshirt, and sweatpants were soaked. But the clothes kind of suctioned to my skin and seemed to give me a little warmth. Which was lucky. The water was the roughest it had been—the cold front was whipping up a storm. The waves were pounding, and it was getting windier. Will and I kept shaking Marquis, saying, "Hold on, hold on, it's going to be all right. It's going to be light soon. They'll find us."

For the most part, we were able to stay on the boat. Will

stood to the right of the motor where he could hold himself up on the swim platform and the trim tab and the little ladder. Corey, though, had begun to struggle more and more. He was completely in the water now, dangling from the back of the boat, his life jacket holding his head and upper body above water. When I could hear him, it sounded like he was blowing bubbles. He was quiet, just, *brrrrrr*, and then it was like he got a big chill: all of a sudden he'd let out a scream, and it would be amplified times a thousand. The waves were nailing him against the boat. When he lost his grip, he would struggle to swim back to the stern or he'd grab my foot or Will's hand, and we'd pull him back. It was agony.

Marquis was growing limp. He would slide down from my grasp, and I had to keep adjusting him. I was trying to lean back a little and keep him pressed against me so that his back wouldn't hit against the motor. I held him as my legs were cramping and my shins were burning. Holding on with my toes put constant pressure on my shins, like a real bad shin splint.

Waves continued blind-siding us from behind, pitching us forward and into the motor. Marquis would revive and try to get away. His eyes were moving side to side, rolling back in his head. He continued to foam at the mouth. It was almost completely dark, but there was enough light to see his face. He wasn't responding, but I kept trying to reassure him, even if I wasn't sure I believed it myself: "Marquis, don't worry. You're gonna see Rebekah and Delaney soon. You're gonna be fine. The girls called the Coast Guard. They'll be here soon."

Paula Oliveira, Nick Schuyler's girlfriend, was away at a dance competition all day Saturday in Lakeland, Florida. She got home about nine thirty or ten at night, fell asleep, and woke up about 12:30 or 1:00 A.M. It was now Sunday, March 1. Nick wasn't home. Mildly concerned, Paula called his cell phone number. It went right to voice mail. Next she tried Will's phone. It rang once and then also went to voice mail.

At 1:27 the Coast Guard station in St. Petersburg, Florida, received notification that a twenty-one-foot Everglades model fishing boat was overdue. The caller was Brian Miller, a friend of Marquis Cooper's. Miller had spoken to Rebekah Cooper, Marquis's wife. He told the Coast Guard that the boat had departed the Seminole Boat Ramp in Clearwater, apparently headed to fish at a dive wreck fifty nautical miles west of Clearwater Pass. Cooper, the owner, had just rebuilt the motor, the caller said. And he had very little maritime experience. The caller said mistakenly that there were two other passengers on board, and that they had no maritime experience.

Cooper's vehicle was described as a 2004 silver Chevrolet Silverado with a lifted suspension and a twenty-one-foot, double-axle trailer. The Coast Guard station made multiple calls on VHF Channel Sixteen—the international distress frequency—for the overdue vessel but got negative results. That far offshore, Cooper's boat was outside of the range of the Coast Guard's communications towers.

The St. Petersburg Coast Guard station handles thirteen hundred to fourteen hundred search-and-rescue cases each year. Its sector extends along Florida's Gulf Coast from seventy miles southeast of Tallahassee to the Everglades. A call that someone was overdue did not immediately result in the sending out of rescue craft. There was a checklist of questions that must first be asked and answered:

Where were the boaters headed? When were they expected back? What was their normal routine? Did they go far offshore? Stay close?

"It's not unusual for us to go to the boat ramp, and they could be back having dinner or having a couple drinks in a bar somewhere and having never bothered to call the wife and say, 'We're stopping off,'" said Captain Timothy M. Close, commander of the St. Petersburg Coast Guard sector.

Four officers were on watch in the Coast Guard station, one monitoring communications, three in the adjacent command center that contained television screens and maps of the Gulf Coast. The St. Petersburg station contacted the Pinellas County Sheriff's Department. It requested that a deputy be sent to the Seminole Boat Ramp to see if Cooper's Silverado was still parked there. The sheriff's department contacted the Clearwater Police Department. At 1:58 a police officer arrived at the ramp, found the truck and trailer, and forwarded the license tag: U565ED. He was asked to leave a note for Cooper, asking him to call the Coast Guard office in St. Petersburg.

Every fifteen minutes, the Coast Guard kept making calls on the international distress frequency. Each call brought no reply. Coast Guard officials began to obtain cell phone numbers for the men reportedly on the overdue boat. The corresponding phone companies were contacted. One number belonged to a Sprint caller. The Coast Guard asked Sprint for the phone's GPS position. A check was made and it was determined that the number belonged to a land line, not a cell phone.

A request was made for a Coast Guard C-130 Hercules turboprop aircraft. It would fly directly over the dive wreck area where the boat was supposed to be fishing. It was to make a search along a series of parallel tracks that would cover an area twenty miles by thirty miles.

It was also recommended that a forty-seven-foot motor lifeboat be sent due west of Clearwater Pass. The motor lifeboats were designed originally for heavy surf on the West Coast, Captain Close said, and were self-righting, meaning they could roll over and pop back upright. They were meant to handle gale force seas in daylight or darkness and were the safest boat the Coast Guard had for such conditions. Two coxswains were requested to navigate the boat in such roiling waters.

At 2:37, seventy minutes after the Everglades boat had

been declared overdue, the case was upgraded from alert to distress.

"The weather was bad and that ratcheted it up from the start," Captain Close said. "They had never been this late before. Sometimes they fished near shore at dark, but they had never stayed out after dark that far before. At that point, no one had come in contact with these guys since they left. It was coming up on twenty hours. They always called. They had cell phones. They had gone out fifty miles before and now it was windy, with rough seas. The water temperature was sixty-fourish. We were very concerned about that."

If the overdue boaters had been tossed into the Gulf, they would have become susceptible to swallowing large amounts of seawater. This could lead to a poisonous imbalance of sodium in the blood, the leaching of water from cells, and eventually delirium, seizures, a heart attack, and ultimately death from dehydration.

In the water, the boaters would also have quickly become susceptible to hypothermia as their body temperatures dropped below 95 degrees. Blood vessels in the arms and legs would begin constricting, rerouting blood to the body's core to protect the heart, lungs, and brain with sufficient heat. Shivering would progress to clumsiness of the hands, quick and shallow breathing, blue lips, confusion, slurred speech, and irrational and confrontational behavior.

Ironically, the younger and fitter a person was, the more he might be vulnerable to hypothermia, with less body fat to provide insulation from the cold. According to a military survival guide, an average twenty-five-year-old man, immersed in water that was 65 degrees, could be expected to remain functional for 9.9 hours and to survive for 15 hours. By contrast, a fifty-year-old man, likely with more body fat for insulation, could be expected to remain functional for 11.6 hours and to survive for 17.6 hours.

"Someone in their twenties is probably going to be in the best shape of their life," said Lieutenant Bruno Baltazar, chief of the command center at the St. Petersburg Coast Guard station. "But having more muscle is going to weigh you down. You're going to have less flotation, which means you're going to have to tread water a lot harder to stay afloat. Someone older is going to have a little more insulation. Not only are you conserving some of that heat, but you're also able to float a little better.

"That's one of the downsides of being in great shape. Especially with someone who plays football, endurance isn't your best bet. It's a sport where you have short stints of rapid movement and then you come to a stop. When you have to tread water for hours on end, that's where having stamina and longevity would come in."

In some cases, incoherent victims of hypothermia began removing their clothes. The phenomenon was not precisely understood. According to one theory, paralysis of nerves in the blood vessels led them to dilate and begin to fill, thus creating a sense of warmth in victims. According to another theory, as the muscles that constricted the blood vessels began to tire, the vessels relaxed and widened, again creating a sense of warmth. Victims then began to shed their clothes, a phenomenon known as paradoxical undressing, which only hastened the dropping of the core body temperature.

"It represents the last effort of the victim and is followed almost immediately by unconsciousness and death," according to a 1979 study published in the *Journal of Forensic Sciences*.

German scientists, writing in the *International Journal of Legal Medicine* in 1995, had also detected a phenomenon in which victims in the final stages of hypothermia exhibited a primitive burrowing-type behavior in order to protect themselves. The behavior was similar to that of hibernating animals, and could lead victims to crawl under beds or into closets indoors or to tunnel into piles of leaves or culverts outdoors. The behavior was known as terminal burrowing.

It was urgent for the Coast Guard to begin searching for Cooper and the other fishermen. "That was an awful long way to be out in that size boat with only a single engine," Captain Close said. But where were the boaters exactly? Formulating a computerized search program was the equivalent of dropping ten thousand rubber ducks into the water and figuring out the probabilities of where they would most likely drift according to the effects of wind, waves, and currents, Captain Close said. Much was still unknown about the overdue Everglades boat. Was the boat upright or had it capsized? Were the fishermen still aboard? Had they gone into the water? If so, had they stayed with the boat? Drifting boats tended to be influenced more by wind than humans, who were more directly affected by current, Captain Close said. Sometimes the wind and current moved in the same direction. Sometimes they did not.

If the boat was overturned and still afloat, much less of it would be visible to searchers than an upright boat. The Coast Guard would be looking for a fingernail of a white hull amid hundreds of thousands of whitecaps in heaving

seas. The moon phase was between a new moon and the
first quarter. What little light that existed was being
smothered by the cloud cover of a storm-churning cold
front. There was one other bit of troubling news. The boat
had sent no distress signal. Apparently it was not equipped
with an emergency position-indicating radio beacon, or
EPIRB. The devices, which can be operated manually
or can automatically activate when a boat overturns,
were cylindrical or cube-shaped, and cost an average
of about five hundred dollars. They sent out a unique
signal to the international satellite system for search and
rescue, providing an immediate location of the boat and
identification of the craft and its user.

"If they had had one, there wouldn't have been search,
there would have been rescue," Captain Close said. "I'll
never say these guys were stupid. They were college-
educated, intelligent guys. They were inexperienced
boaters, and they were in an element they weren't prepared
for. They didn't have a good sense, like very many boaters,
how bad things can actually be and how isolated they can
actually be when they're that far from the shore. It's the
equivalent of taking your light jacket and saying, 'I'm going
to go climb Mount McKinley.'"

At 2:38 Miller, the Cooper family friend, called the
Coast Guard back. He said that a handheld GPS device had
been located belonging to Marquis. The device should have
the coordinates indicating the exact position where Cooper
usually went to fish. The caller said he would instruct
Cooper's wife how to power up the GPS device and scroll to
the relevant information.

It was the Coast Guard's sense, Captain Close said, that
Miller had helped Cooper buy the boat, often accompanied
him on the boat, and often operated the boat.

The missing fishermen may have been in the water for hours already. That was hugely significant in terms of survivability. "If they had flipped and we had gotten immediate initial notification, we still would have had an hour or two of daylight," Captain Close said. "It wouldn't have taken us an hour to go from alert to distress. You've got to be able to help yourself. These guys were just unprepared. It's not atypical for a lot of boaters out there. It's 'I've got the money, I'm buying a boat, I want to go fast, and I want to drink beer while I'm doing it.' "

At 2:47 the Coast Guard issued an Urgent Marine Information Broadcast, informing other vessels that a search-and-rescue mission was under way and asking them to reply if they had heard a Mayday signal from a boat in distress.

The Cooper family friend called the St. Petersburg Coast Guard station again at 2:53. He passed along a GPS position of 27°58'09" N and 083°42'01" W. This was about ten miles south of the plotted shipwreck site, Cooper's supposed destination. The search area had now grown larger and thus less precise, more uncertain, more complicated.

The adjusted coordinates were transmitted to the C-130 Hercules turboprop that was set to fly over the area. Some confusion followed about the Hercules, according to the official Coast Guard report. Two planes actually were available, but the first one developed engine problems and never got airborne. A second C-130 finally launched over the Gulf at three o'clock in the morning, flying at 1,000 feet at 140 miles an hour. The C-130 arrived on the scene shortly but began experiencing technical problems. It could not get its radar to operate in the eight-foot seas.

"Radar doesn't see through water," Captain Close said.

"When you have small waves, you can adjust the radar so sea clutter gets ignored. You can suppress everything that appears to be one- to two-foot waves. When you have eight- to ten-foot seas, if you suppress the radar to the point that you can't see anything smaller than waves that high, what's the use of having it on? You're looking for a boat that's really small to begin with, even if it's floating."

At 4:40 A.M. the Coast Guard contacted AT&T and confirmed Corey Smith's cell phone number. AT&T tried to get a GPS position from the iPhone but failed.

At 5:50, the C-130 reported that stormy conditions allowed the plane to effectively search only 40 percent of its intended tracking area of 600 square miles. Sixteen minutes later, a request was made to launch an HH-60 Jayhawk helicopter.

The C-130 Hercules still had its forward-looking infrared system available, which allowed pilots to distinguish a warm object, such as a boat engine or a human body, from the cold background of the water. But by six in the morning, as the cold front continued to move in, bad weather made the infrared system useless. The C-130 reduced the spacing between its parallel search tracks from eight miles to three miles. Still it was basically flying blind for about half of its intended search area.

"They essentially searched nothing," said the official Coast Guard report.

Paula Oliveira kept sleeping fitfully, waking every thirty or forty minutes. She kept trying Nick's cell phone, but the same thing happened each time: straight to voice mail. She got up and sat outside on the deck of their house in the Carrollwood section of Tampa. Nick had never wanted her to worry. If he was out with the guys and would be late, he would always call. This time he hadn't. She tried to stay positive. Maybe they got in late from fishing and they were so tired that they grabbed something to eat at Marquis's house and fell asleep. She kept praying for that scenario. She didn't want to sound like a crazy girlfriend, so she tried not to appear upset in her phone messages to Nick: "Hey Babe, it's late. I'm just seeing what you guys are doing and when you'll be home. Call me as soon as you can."

She still didn't think they were in big trouble. She knew they had taken beer. Maybe they had been cited for drinking or maybe they had caught an illegal fish. The more Paula thought about it, she knew that didn't feel right. She kept trying Nick's cell phone. By three thirty or four, she cried as she left her message, "Babe, please call."

Now I could see that Corey had developed some of the same symptoms as Marquis. It was about five on Sunday morning. He was floating in the water at the back of the boat. He started rambling a lot, making moaning sounds. Will and I would call his name, but he wouldn't answer until we had yelled out four or five times.

Then all of a sudden, Corey got this desperate energy. It was like he had awakened and realized he needed to get on the boat right away. I was still sitting on the hull, straddling the motor as Marquis lay across my lap. Corey pulled on Marquis's legs, grabbing for whatever he could to get himself out of the water. He had this look on his face. He looked mad and mean. I knew something was going on. Maybe this was a last-ditch effort to save himself. I guess the cold was starting to take hold. We had been in the water twelve hours.

Mentally, Corey wasn't there. That was clear to me now. It wasn't him, just like it wasn't Marquis in my arms. Corey was the nicest guy—the easiest guy to get along with. Now he was getting nasty and physical and trying to get on the boat. He'd try for ten or fifteen seconds, go lifeless, and then try again to get out of the water.

"No, no, stop, there's no place to go!" Will and I began yelling at Corey. "Stop, stop!"

It seemed like it went on for about a half hour. And it kept getting worse. "You can't, there's no room, stop," we told Corey, but we weren't getting through to him. He was pulling on Marquis, at first not really saying anything, then shouting, "Bitch, bitch!" He was really getting aggressive, just random actions. I had never seen Corey mad or heard him say anything mean about anybody. He was a jokester. This wasn't him, not the real Corey.

Around this time, we heard a noise, then saw a light. I thought it was a helicopter. Later, I would learn that the first Coast Guard helicopter did not reach the search area until after sunrise. And my sister would say I told her that I saw a light that turned away, as if it came from a boat. Could my timing be off? Could the Coast Guard report be wrong by an hour or so? Could a helicopter have come and not been included in the official report? Could it have been the forty-seven-foot motor lifeboat that I saw? A plane? Was I hallucinating? Did I imagine it after being in the water, freezing, for half a day? I don't think so. I know I saw something.

The helicopter or boat or plane—I'm certain it was a helicopter, it seemed so vivid, you could see the shape of it—probably got within five hundred yards of us. There was a spotlight, much bigger than what you'd see in a theater. It seemed so close. This was our shot to get out of this. There was definitely someone moving the light around. You could see the waves now, a lot of white crashing down—it seemed like waves came from every single angle possible. You would get pounded from the back, your body slamming against the motor, and then another wave would come and hurl you the other way.

Will and I were telling Corey, "They're here. Be quiet, they're here!"

Marquis was completely out of it. He was fighting a little bit, but not nearly like before.

"They're here!" I told him. "You're going to see your family. The families are waiting at home. Your little girl is waiting for you."

I envisioned it the way you see it on TV, the helicopter dropping a basket and saving us on a stormy night. "Thank you, God, thank you!"

The light got closer. The beam passed over us, a sliver of white boat in a sea of white. "Oh my God, oh my God!" we yelled. We screamed and waved, "Help, we're down here! Help!"

Will still had that cushion strapped to his back, the one he found under the boat. It was white and a faded brown. He took it off and waved it like a towel. You could hear the waves crashing so loud, the waves and the wind. Just to hear one another speak, we had to yell twice as loud. It was like the beach, one wave finishes and another comes crashing in—relentless, unending.

Corey seemed to revive himself for a minute. "They see us?" he asked. He took his watch and tried to press the dial, hoping it would light up and someone could see the dim flash. But the battery must have been dying. The dial would flash for a millisecond and go dark.

We had the two flares that Will had found under the boat in the canopy over the center console. The ones we stashed in Marquis's swimsuit. They were like Roman candles. We had tried to read the directions earlier by the light of a cell phone. Will ripped the top off of them and pounded the bottom of the flares on his hand or on the hull. He couldn't get them lit.

"Are you doing it right?" I asked.

"Yeah, they're soaked," he said.

We thought the flares were supposed to be waterproof.

Will screamed "Fuck!" as loud as he could.

We watched the light as it moved away. At one point it seemed to be barely moving, just hovering, and then it started moving faster. We could see it, but it was not near us now. The light had come across the boat, then moved a few yards away from us; then it was a mile away, and then we couldn't see it. And we couldn't hear the sound of whatever brought the light.

We let out a lot of F-bombs.

"Are you kidding me? How can they not see us?!"

SHORTLY AFTER WE saw the light, Marquis became lifeless. He had gone from being completely restless—fighting and squirming and wriggling and trying to turn, grabbing my head and my neck and trying to flip himself—to not resisting at all. He was completely slack.

Will and I didn't think much about it at first. We thought, okay, he's calming down now. But he hadn't fought at all for about ten minutes. Then I realized that he seemed unconscious. There was no final moan or scream, nothing.

I called his name. "Coop? Coop? You there? Marquis?"

I squeezed him with my arms, an even bigger bear hug than before. Nothing happened. No movement. I shook him, slapped his face.

"You don't want your daughter to grow up without a father," I told him.

Corey kept pulling and tugging on Marquis from the back of the boat. Sometimes he reached over and grabbed Will, who stood at the stern on the other side of the motor. Or Corey lifted his waist or his hips out of the water and seized my life jacket and try to pull at me. Then he would fall back in.

Two of us were now in trouble. I said to Will, "Please tell me you're all right."

I looked right at him.

"I'm okay, don't worry," he said. "I'll be fine."

There was no sarcasm in his voice. I would ask guys when we worked out at the gym if they were okay and they would give you that sarcastic, "Yeah, I'm great!" but through the whole night when I asked Will and Marquis and Corey the same thing, they were not cynical.

I sat on the hull with my right hand on Corey's jacket, trying to keep him tight against the boat so he wouldn't tug at me and Will and Marquis. Working so hard seemed to make me forget about the cold. I had more clothes on than the other guys. Maybe all this work created more body heat and kept my blood flowing. There wasn't time to sit and think about how cold I was and how my muscles were burning. My stomach hurt. I didn't know if it was because I had been sick and was hungry or because I was so afraid.

I told Will that we had to flip Marquis over, turn his face upward. Water might be getting in his mouth.

"I'm not sure if he's conscious," I said. "He's not fighting anymore."

Will and I managed to turn Marquis until he was laying flat on his back, facing the sky. Before, he was facing the front of the boat across my lap. I held Corey with my right hand and held Marquis like a baby now. There was no more need to bear hug him with the same strength. He wasn't fighting me. My left hand was underneath him, kind of underneath his neck. He was sitting on my legs, his left hip against the motor, his right hip against my belly button. My right leg was up, and I folded his legs into my stomach. I was holding deadweight now. That's a terrible thing to say.

Marquis wasn't there. His eyes were shut, he was foaming at the mouth. I slapped his face lightly, telling him, "Keep holding on—we'll be home before you know it."

His neck would droop and his jaw would fall open. I noticed he was getting a little water in his mouth. I told Will, "We've got to shut it." Bracing himself against the motor, his left hand holding Corey's life jacket, Will used his right hand to keep Marquis's head up and his mouth closed. I was holding him like an infant. Randomly, Corey would let go of the boat, and we yelled at him, "Chill, chill—relax—help's here—just a little longer—relax—they're here!"

At one point I got his attention and told Corey to give me his watch so we could keep track of time. I latched it to my life jacket, at my sternum. He started putting his feet on the stern and pulling on my jacket and pushing off the back of the boat. He was showing his teeth now, angry. I could see the look in his eyes—there were like Marquis's eyes. They were going every which way, rolling in the back of his head, like he had some kind of dementia. He was swearing random "Fuck yous!" I had never heard him swear in the couple of months that I had known him. Not angry cursing. Now he was being mean. It wasn't Corey. It was like evil Corey, like Corey's demon.

Corey would bend his legs like a frog against the back of the boat, and then he would push away, jumping backward. He was tearing and yanking at Marquis, grabbing and pulling on me, my jacket, and then he would let go completely.

"Grab on!" I told him. "Hold on to the boat!"

About ten minutes after we flipped Marquis over, I told Will to check his pulse. He was limp in my arms, and I feared the worst.

Will leaned his ear down and tried to hear Marquis's breathing. The water and the wind were so loud. It was a whistling wind, a consistent blow with random strong gusts. The water was flying in and smashing us. I wore a cross on a chain around my neck, and I put the cross in my mouth. I sat there and prayed. "Please God, please God."

Will said, "I can't hear him breathing."

Marquis did seem to have a pulse, though. Will felt his neck.

He must have checked him for a good minute. Waves were crashing, Marquis's feet were sliding down. I was losing my grip on his head. We kept having to pull him up into my lap.

Meanwhile, Corey continued yanking on me and Marquis. Eventually, he started pulling on Will. "You got him?" I asked Will.

My left hand was still under Marquis's neck. Will had Corey, so I took my right hand and pumped Marquis's chest to make sure his heart was still beating. Corey really started fighting. He would struggle for about ten seconds, then he would go lifeless. Then he'd fight for a minute and go lifeless again. Then he would really fight—"Bitch, come on bitch!" Will was holding on to him, and he went at Will with both hands. He almost jumped on his neck, like a headlock, knocking Will off the boat. In the water, Will was able to get away from Corey for a minute.

"Stop, no!" I yelled at Corey.

I stayed on the hull, my legs around the motor, holding Marquis, praying that he was alive. Will grabbed Corey and held on to him in the crashing waves, about five feet from the boat. They got near the stern, and I reached and grasped Corey's life jacket with my right hand. He was kind of sagging now, not holding on to anything. I tried to prop Marquis's head up with my left hand, doing what I could to wipe the foam off his mouth. "They're going to be here soon," I told Marquis again. "They're already looking for us. It's a matter of time."

Will returned to the boat and helped me take hold of Corey. "Don't let go of him," I said.

Corey tugged at me, trying to pull himself up. I said, "Corey, stop, you're hurting me." He was choking me, grabbing my life jacket. My neck felt like it had rug burn. Corey kept yanking and jerking, trying to hoist himself up, a 265-pound man having a delirious temper tantrum. He probably did that twenty times.

"The sun is going to come up soon," I said, trying to calm him. "It'll be daylight. They'll see us."

I asked Will to check Marquis's pulse again.

He put his finger on his neck. He leaned in to listen.

"I don't know," Will said. "I can't find it."

I tried to stay positive, even though I feared the inevitable.

"He's alive, he's fine," I said.

My right hand was burning now, holding on to Corey. He began flinging himself again, squatting against the boat and trying to jump away. Over and over. I was getting jolted. A couple of times Corey pulled on Will's jacket, or whatever he could get ahold of. Then he would grab my jacket.

Will would let go of Corey and try to stay out of reach for a few moments so Corey couldn't tug or choke him. Meanwhile, I kept holding Corey, while keeping Marquis balanced in my lap. I asked Will a couple times, "You all right?"

His answer was short, serious.

"Yeah, yeah," he would say.

"Good," I told him once, "because I can't do this without you."

Not only had we taken care of ourselves, but now two of us were helping four people. I got to the point where I felt like I couldn't hold on to both Marquis and Corey for another second. Marquis was completely inert, and I didn't think I could keep holding a 215-pound guy, using one arm and one leg, while I also restrained an even heavier man who was trying to pogo-stick himself away from me.

Every muscle I had was burning—my shoulders, upper back, lower back. The rug burn on my neck was getting bad. My hands were so pruned and battered. I still had my cotton gloves on, but at that point all but two or three fingers were torn from banging into the boat and the motor and trying to hold on to those two guys. Blood seeped through the gashes in my gloves. The motor had plenty of solid, hard edges. The sharp propeller was nearly in my face. I was sitting on the keel, and I kept trying to shift my weight because the ridge of the keel ran right up the crack of my ass.

Both of my legs were uncomfortable. My right hip flexor was gone.
I was cramping in my hip, my groin, my feet. I kept trying to move
my toes. I was in so much frickin' pain. I was pumping my chest,
shrugging my shoulders, squeezing my abs. I kept telling Will to do
the same thing. Whether he did or not, I don't know.

I think it was close to six now. Marquis had been unconscious
for a while. Corey was thrashing. I kept telling him, "They'll be
here in ten minutes." I said anything to try to calm him down.

Corey and Will continued their sad tug of war. Corey would
pull Will into the water, and Will would let go of him to get free
for a second. Then they would just float behind the boat. Will held
Corey with his left hand and tried to hold on to the motor or some
other part of the boat with his right hand. Corey pulled on the
cushion Will had on his back. He yanked on Will's arm. Quite a
few times, Will floated for what seemed like ten minutes, holding
on to the boat, but completely in the water, the cushion still on his
back.

I kept looking at the watch I had taken from Corey and saying
to him, "The sun's coming up—they're on the way!"

Marquis remained limp. I didn't know if he was alive or not.
Corey was the opposite of Marquis. Marquis's fights had been
longer and more frequent, but they died down. Corey's were more
sporadic at first, but as it got closer to dawn, they got more frequent, stronger, and more consistent, with more swearing, more
meanness.

He wouldn't say more than a few words, like "Come here,
bitch!" There was a terrible look in his eyes. They seemed completely bloodshot and real wide. He would let out loud grunts.

"They're going to be here real soon," I said to Corey, and I
would tell Marquis, "Coop, hold on a little longer, just a little
longer—we'll be home soon."

It was not yet light. Marquis was just laying across me, not moving. Will checked him a third time. He shook his head. He couldn't find a pulse.

"I don't know man," Will said. "I don't think he's here. I think he's gone."

I held on to Corey and tapped Marquis's face, trying to wake him. Corey ripped at me or Will or Marquis. A couple times he got away from me, and Will held on to him. Or I pushed him off of me and then grabbed him again quickly because he was choking me. The strap burn on my neck from my life jacket was getting worse. Corey was really jerking at Marquis now, and I had to squeeze Marquis tighter to keep him on the boat. I was terrified. Waves were still smashing in. Now I thought it might be drizzling. It was hard to tell, because it felt like that all the time.

Facing away from the boat, I continued to ask Will whether the bow was still up and out of the water. Sometimes he said it looked the same; sometimes he said it didn't look good.

About now, we knew that Marquis had probably died. I was pumping his chest a little harder than before. I put my mouth to his mouth, but the waves were so rough I couldn't give him CPR effectively. Will couldn't do it, either. We were trying to hold Corey at the same time, and it was too much. My hope was that Marquis was still alive. They'll get here, they'll take him first, then come back for Corey and worry about us later, I said to myself. I guess I was in denial. I couldn't let myself believe the worst.

The waves were probably nine or ten feet high, coming from every angle. It was choppy, a bad storm. I was freezing. My orange jacket had a drawstring and I tried to pull it tight to my body. But a wave would come from the backside and shoot right up my jacket, from the top of my butt to the top of my neck. It felt like the first time we went into the water, like needles. I would shout, "Oh my God!" with my teeth clinched.

Will checked Marquis again and said, "Dude, I think he's

gone." I didn't want to answer, because I didn't want to believe it.

Marquis had been unconscious for what seemed like more than an hour. Now it was after six. We were waiting. We knew we had a better chance of being found in daylight.

I told Corey what I had said before: "Hold on, they're going to be here soon." And to Marquis: "Please God, stay with us, Coop."

Corey was jumping again, hurtling from the boat like he was starting a backstroke race in a pool. He kept pulling me, and my endurance was shot.

I told Will about Corey, "You better hold on to him—I can't."

Now Corey began catapulting away from the boat at a forty-five-degree angle. Will would have needed another three feet on his arm to hold on—he was already waist-high out of the water now, still trying to keep Marquis's listless head up with one hand. I didn't want to believe it, but Will was right. Marquis was gone. We couldn't get a pulse. There had been no sign of life for more than an hour. He was gone. He was dead.

It was about six fifteen. Corey was either at full throttle or nothing—just floating in the water or fighting and ripping at my life jacket. He was out of Will's reach, so it was up to me to hold on to him. I thought that if Corey's life jacket ever came off, we would lose him, too.

Will and I kept trying to calm Corey down.

The helicopter's gone to refuel, I told him. They would come back when it was light out. I kept telling Marquis to hang on a little longer, just a little longer, but these were just words, as empty and lifeless as he was.

Why, God? I kept thinking. Everything said by everybody seemed to have the word *God* in it as that first night went on. Corey and Marquis were more religious than me, but we all said the same thing: "I don't get it, God. Why me? Please, God!"

I had never gotten emotional until now. There was too much

going on. I was scared for my life. But now I knew I couldn't hold on to both Marquis and Corey anymore. Every ounce of muscle in my body was shot.

"I don't know what to do," I told Will. "I'm going to have to let go of one of them. Otherwise I'll lose both of them."

We decided to take Marquis's life jacket off because Will was still wearing the seat cushion. He took it off his back and it floated away in seconds.

"Oh shit," Will said.

He quickly put on Marquis's life jacket while I held on to Corey, who was still being rough. He got hold of Will again, and Will went into the water. "No, no!" I yelled.

Corey was making grunting sounds, almost like he wanted to wrestle. He would grab Will and try to pull him under. He kept yanking on Marquis, and Marquis's head kept slipping down, his head falling to my waist. His legs were now completely in the water.

"Stop, stop!" I yelled at Corey. "They'll be here soon!"

I said to Will again, "I can't hold both of them."

Will tried to keep one hand on Corey, but it was hard. Corey would grab him and try to pull himself forward. Then Will would have to let go of Marquis and hold the motor with one hand to fend off Corey.

Will and I went back and forth.

"I don't know what to do," I kept saying.

I had to make a decision. It was just a matter of time before I would lose my grip on Corey and he would break free.

"You're going to have to let Marquis go," Will said.

"There's no way," I said.

"You're gonna have let him go."

I struggled with it, but I knew Will was right. I had already lost Marquis. I knew he was dead. Corey was still alive.

Will said again, "You gotta let him go."

Corey pulled Marquis by the legs with both hands. Now Marquis's whole lower half was in the water, his body getting slammed by ten-foot choppy waves as Corey tried to thrust himself off the boat.

"I don't know, man," I said to Will. "I don't know."

And then I told Marquis, "I love you, Coop. I'll see you again someday. I'll protect your family."

I let Marquis slide slowly into the water. I told him that I loved him another five or six times. I held on to his wrist with my left hand while holding Corey with my right. Ninety-nine percent of him was in the water now; he was facing the front of the boat, very limp. I felt his body. It was cold and hard.

I kept telling Marquis that I loved him. Then I let him go. It was by far the hardest thing I ever had to do. I watched his body slowly fall away. His head kind of floated in the water, down and off to the side. I watched him a few seconds as his body slowly sank. I shook my head and kept telling him that I loved him. His body was at a slight angle. He drifted away, and within a few seconds I didn't see him anymore. My face hurt and my eyes burned as I tried to hold back the tears.

WILL DIDN'T SAY anything as Marquis floated away. Then Corey started fighting again. Even though I no longer held Marquis, I couldn't get both my arms around Corey, not with the motor in the way.

It wasn't more than a few minutes later when Corey began trying to take off his life jacket. He seemed confused. He would try to lift it up and pull it over his head. Will would reach over and yank it back down.

Then Corey tried to jump away from the boat probably four

times in ten seconds. Not straight back, but at a forty-five-degree angle—he would bend his legs and catapult himself. I called to Will, "I'm going to lose him!"

Corey positioned himself near the motor and somehow he stood up, grabbed on to me, and pulled himself up. He looked right into my eyes and said, "Fuck you—I'm a kill you!" He said it again. His eyes were wild.

That wasn't Corey. I knew it. I didn't take it personally. A second later, he jumped to my left across the motor as I straddled it. My right arm cut across the propeller. I felt a sharp pain near my wrist, and my immediate reaction was to yank my hand backward. I lost him. I didn't mean to, but I lost Corey.

I screamed, "Will, grab him!"

Will jumped from the stern into the water and tried to grab Corey, but he was getting away, and Will couldn't risk straying too far from the boat in rough water. Corey got away a final time, gripped his life jacket, and jerked it over his head. It remained attached for a moment by the lower strap, but then Corey ripped the jacket over his head and let go of it.

"Corey, Corey!" we screamed. At this point, he was probably ten feet away from the boat. It was almost like he did a swan dive. His arms didn't come out of the water, but his head went down and he did a front roll; his sneakers went straight into the air. He seemed to be ninety degrees vertical. He kicked straight down until we couldn't see him anymore.

I screamed, "Corey, no, no, no, please!"

I yelled so loud and my mouth was so dry it felt like I was shredding my throat.

Will was screaming, too, "No, no, oh God, no!"

In a few seconds, we couldn't see Corey anymore. He went under and never resurfaced. For a second, I saw his sneakers, and then I didn't. Then I saw them again. Finally, they were gone for good.

"Why, God, why?!" I screamed.

About fifteen minutes after we let go of Marquis, we had lost Corey. We were stunned. They were such calm, cool guys. And then they had become someone else, something else, and now they were gone.

It was getting lighter out, about six thirty or six forty-five.

Over the next few hours, Will and I would ask each other, "Why would he do that? Why?"

At 6:38 on this Sunday morning, the Coast Guard suggested that relatives be told to check their missing boaters' credit cards to see if they had been used in recent hours. It was also suggested that a search be made closer to shore. "Being that these guys are inexperienced, don't look just at fifty miles offshore," a Coast Guard dispatch said. "There might be a possibility that they wisened [sic] up and stayed close to shore. At least within visual of land. Find out their departure point. Park? Marina? Home? How much fuel onboard? It might be worth considering getting the story out to media earlier than later—more people on the lookout both on land and water."

Just after sunrise, at 7:09, the first Jayhawk helicopter was launched. It reached the search area at 7:45. At 7:10, the forty-seven-foot motor lifeboat arrived at the GPS coordinates provided by Marquis Cooper's friend from a handheld device. Seas were now running eight to ten feet, with some rising to twelve feet. The wind was blowing thirty miles an hour. Visibility was half a mile.

"That's an E-ticket ride at Disney World," said Captain Timothy Close, commander of the St. Petersburg Coast Guard station, explaining how rough a trip the motor lifeboat experienced.

The initial search by the boat brought no luck in the battering seas.

"They were looking out the window and a good percentage of the time they were just looking at water moving past them," Captain Close said of the motor lifeboat. "When they got back, the boat was okay, but the crew was shot. They were in the bag. We had to send them home, probably with a couple Nuprin and an ice pack or two."

By 9:24 in the morning, a second C-130 turboprop had still not been launched, apparently delayed by the weather. "Our command is very unhappy with the response time," said a dispatch from an impatient Coast Guard official.

The initial three-hour helicopter search for the missing boat and boaters also proved futile.

It was dawn now on March 1, very overcast. There were only two of us now. I sat on the hull, and Will was to my left, standing on the swim platform or a trim tab. I had lost two friends, NFL players, guys who seemed indestructible. If we were to have any hope for ourselves, it would come now with sunrise. In daylight, the searchers should have an easier time seeing us. We watched the waves form in the distance. They were consistent ten-footers, choppy. But at least we were able to see what was coming at us.

A white mist surrounded us, and it started to rain—it was pouring. But in a way that was okay. I turned my head up and opened my mouth to get some fresh water. I kept my mouth open thirty seconds at a time. I tasted salt and grittiness from my teeth. I felt like they were filing down from chattering all the time.

At this point, we had been in the water about fifteen hours. We had been awake more than a full day. I was starving and thirsty. My mouth was nasty, dry. I was nauseous. I felt my stomach. I felt thin already. I weighed 240, and was in great shape, but I could tell I was getting thinner. I had thrown up breakfast the day before when I got seasick. I couldn't hold anything down after that. The last real meal I ate, Will's mother's pasta recipe, had been on Friday night, about thirty-six hours ago.

By eight in the morning we had been thrown off the boat a couple times. I was getting plowed. My body would go flying off, a complete 360. My legs would slam against the motor, and my back would pound against the hull.

Will and I decided to position ourselves on the hull. I straddled the motor, and he bear-hugged me from behind. It was like we were riding a Jet Ski, but there was nothing for him to hold on to but me. When we'd get thrown off, we'd climb back on and switch positions. The person in the front did 99 percent of the work, holding on to the motor and gripping with his feet. Soon I was in excruciating pain. A wave would come from behind and nail us and we would rocket forward, more than 450 pounds between us, and my balls would slam against the motor. They were the hardest hits I had taken, way harder than on a football field. It happened so many times, over and over. We would pound against the motor and I would feel a sharp pain in my crotch, then a nauseous feeling, like I wanted to vomit.

A lot of time we were coughing and gagging from the water. My nose was running. We both had colds. We were spitting, and the one in front would get hit with loogies, or one person would put his finger to his nose and blow a snot rocket. We didn't care. The waves washed it away in a minute.

When we sat like that, one guy bear-hugging the other, there wasn't a whole lot of talking. We would watch for the waves and yell, "Hold on, hold on!" and we would lean in and brace ourselves.

"Hey," Will said at one point.

"Hey," I said. "You all right?"

His reply was tinged with fear. There was a sad tone to his voice, which was choked up. "I'm not going to make it through another night," Will said. "No way."

"Don't worry," I told him. "You won't have to. They're going to find us today."

I tried to brush it off, but I got scared, too. I felt sick to my stomach. Will always had an idea or a plan. He was the one who swam under the boat to get the life jackets. We were best friends. If he didn't have hope, how could I? There had been four of us, and the cold and the salt water had gotten to Marquis and Corey. Now it was just me and Will. We could climb a little more out of the water, the two of us, bear-hugging each other, creating some heat. Still, we were worried about dehydration and the cold. We hadn't eaten. Even after I saw two pro athletes not make it, even after one guy died in my arms and the other guy got away and died minutes later, I still never thought I was going to die. Then Will said what he said, and it began to sink in. Death had just happened in my lap. And it might happen again.

It was storming. The rain felt like it was coming horizontal. It was painful, like BBs to the face. The sky was the color of dishwater. It almost looked foggy. Our visibility was very low. We knew we were drifting in a strong current, but we had no idea if we had drifted five miles one way or ten miles the other way. We felt like the current was pulling us every which way.

Will and I worked well together when we could see the waves in front of us. "Hold on, hold on!" we would yell. If a swell came from the side, we would scream, "One-two-three, lean, lean!" and we would shoulder into the wave to help us stay on the hull, almost like we were on a motorcycle taking a turn. Sometimes, even if we leaned in, it didn't matter. Thousands of pounds of churning water would collapse on us and we couldn't hold on. Or we would lean left or right and a wave would surprise us from behind and send us flying over the motor.

As before, the waves swamping us from behind were the worst. We couldn't always see or anticipate them, and then we would be thrown off the boat. You would come up and take another wave in the face and start choking on water. Sometimes it was a full minute before you could grab the boat again. This happened for hours.

Early in the morning, the waves definitely changed form. They were choppy at first, eight to ten feet, and as the day went on, the waves came together into swells that were fifteen feet tall. I had been in big waves before in Lake Erie, seven- to eight-footers, but when you are in fifteen-foot waves, you have a completely different view. It's one thing to be in a boat that's upright in the water, and another thing to be on a capsized boat or floating in the water in a life jacket. When you can see, feel, taste all fifteen feet, it's a lot different. When a wave comes at you, it's a lot bigger. You see it like a dark mound. We would go up and up and up and then it seemed like we were at the top and it would flatten out and then we would seem to go up more. And then the wave would pass and you could see the back of it. The front was not as steep as the back. You would fall and fall and fall into the pit of the wave. The valley. You could feel it in your stomach. It was not as fast as a roller coaster, but it was like the first drop on one.

Why is this happening to me? I asked myself all day. Why me? Please, God!

Every time the boat came down off one of those big waves, particularly in the afternoon, it would go completely underwater. We had to brace ourselves. We knew we were going under and that the boat was going under. We would take a deep breath and hold it for a few seconds. This happened consistently for hours.

Will and I would have little conversations about the waves or food or wanting something to drink.

"I'm so thirsty," I said once.

"I could go for a milk shake," Will said.

"I could go for a smoothie, my Cavaliers, and my bed," I said.

When a wave came, it wasn't like you got hit by a short burst. It felt like a five-second push and you were just torn off the boat. It was like throwing a bowling ball at toothpicks. Whichever one of us was sitting in the back would turn around to see if a swell was coming. We would try to brace ourselves. But if it was too big or it came from behind and you didn't see it, you would be slammed off the boat in a second. You hit everything, bone against metal, your knees, your head, your whole body bouncing like a ball off a backboard. I was ripped up from my belly button all the way around to my lower back. My groin was raw. My skin was so sensitive from the salt water. My balls were killing me. I was so scared and tired and sick and cold. It was hard and discouraging.

Then you would go from that excruciating pain to being thrown in the water. Sometimes, when a wave came from behind, Will and I flew over the prop—there was nothing to stop us. My stomach would be right on the propeller, like I was body surfing or riding a Boogie board. My hands and the insides of my legs were bleeding from hitting the motor. I hit my head quite a few times.

We must have fallen off the boat fifty times. A wave would come and throw us one foot away or fifteen feet away. Then we would be in the water and another wave would come and I was going, Oh shit, if this one breaks on me, I'll be even further away.

We would go underwater still sitting on the hull, or sometimes we would go off the side and fall even deeper underwater. Quite a few times, I thought the boat might go down and stay down. Constantly, I worried about what would happen if it stayed down and I was still attached to it. Could I get away? Would it suck me down with it?

It was hard not to think, What's the point of getting back on this boat? We had already lost two guys, and the weather was getting worse. Sometimes we went in the water and, exhausted, we didn't attempt to get back on the boat right away. The waves were pounding and we stayed near the boat and tried to keep our heads above water as much as we could. Other times we would get one foot back on the boat, getting a perch, and another wave would come and rip us right off. Sometimes one of us stayed on the boat and the other one flopped in the water. If Will fell in, he would grab my shoulder and pull up, or I would grab him and give an explosive yank. Sometimes I pulled so hard, he would fly over the hull and back in the water on the other side—everything was so slick, there was nothing to grab on to. Other times, I would yank him up and he ended up pulling me in the water with him. It was a constant struggle, hardly a second to relax or catch your breath. Countless times, one of us would get halfway up the boat and fall back in the water, pounded underneath by the wave, and then rise to the top, choking, trying to spit the water out of his mouth.

Getting back on the boat was like trying to throw your leg over the saddle of a horse, except that it was a sharp, jagged, moving, bouncing saddle. And the horse's head wasn't smooth and furry, it was the motor, and it was sharp, metallic, cold, and bucking.

The majority of the work was done by the person sitting in front of the other, grabbing the motor, holding on with his feet. I was working out every day, since it was my job to be in shape, and I was stronger than Will. It felt warmer now that it was daylight. The sun wasn't really out, but it helped Will and me create some kind of body heat as we bear-hugged on the hull. At first it was weird, but there was no other way to hold on. My face felt like sand from being salty.

Paula Oliveira awoke again near dawn, and called the home of Rebekah and Marquis Cooper. But the family was moving, and the number had been disconnected. Paula didn't have Rebekah's cell phone number. So she turned on her laptop computer and Googled the Coast Guard. She called the St. Petersburg station and apologized if she was calling the wrong number, but said that her boyfriend had gone on a fishing trip and had not returned. The Coast Guard officer seem to know Nick's name and hers, too. The officer asked for Nick's date of birth and the spelling of his name. He wanted Paula to describe Nick's features. She said he was 6 feet 2 inches, 240, brown hair, green eyes, a big guy with a muscular build.

"What's this all about?" Paula asked.

The officer explained that Rebekah Cooper, or a family friend, had contacted the Coast Guard and reported the boaters missing. They had been searching for them since about one thirty. Paula began sobbing. She left her number with the Coast Guard and asked them to pass it along to Marquis's wife. Paula then called her father in Fort Lauderdale. She couldn't speak. She was sobbing.

"Paula, what's wrong?" he asked.

"I'm okay," she said. "Nick is missing."

As Paula spoke, her cell phone beeped. It was Rebekah Cooper. She was sitting in her car in the parking lot at the L.A. Fitness where Nick, Marquis, and Corey trained together. Rebekah was waiting for the gym to open at eight. She planned to go inside and ask for a phone number for Paula, who was also a member of the gym. In the meantime, the Coast Guard had passed along Paula's number to Rebekah.

Rebekah's voice was calm and reassuring. The guys probably ran out of gas, or their GPS system wasn't working and they were just drifting, she told Paula. They were probably fine and the Coast Guard would find them. It was daylight now; it would probably take only an hour or two. Paula didn't call Nick's mother. No need to alarm her over nothing.

"I went from pure hysteria to okay," Paula said. "It made sense. Of course that would happen. That gave me peace."

At about eight thirty, Paula made a second call to the Coast Guard in St. Petersburg. Rebekah Cooper had seemed unaware that Will Bleakley had also been on the boat. Paula gave Will's name and birth date to the Coast Guard, along with a description of him—similar to Nick but with darker hair, 6 feet 3 inches, 230—along with his cell phone number.

The morning was chilly. Paula opened the door to let her three dogs out and her feet got cold. She put on a pair of boots and a sweater with her jeans and drove to St. Paul's Catholic Church on North Dale Mabry in Tampa. She had been raised Catholic but did not practice her religion. She arrived just as the service was ending, and walked in crying. People seemed to be staring at her. No one said anything. She went to a pew and sat by herself, asking God to bring Nick, Will, Marquis, and Corey home safely and soon. She stayed for ten minutes and drove to the home of her close friends Nery Tijerino and Kendall Lawson. The Coast Guard called Paula there in late morning, about eleven. She might want to inform Nick's family now, an officer told her. The media were going to be alerted. Before eleven, the Coast Guard would confirm that there were four men missing, not three, and that two of them were NFL players.

"High media interest is expected," said a Coast Guard dispatch.

Except for Nick Schuyler and Will Bleakley, no one could have known yet that the two NFL players were already dead.

Earlier, Paula had become frustrated. "How could they not see them yet?" she wondered about the Coast Guard. Her friend Nery had admonished her, "Paula, you don't know how big an area this is."

When the Coast Guard called her this time in late morning, she asked again what kind of progress it was making. The voice on the other end was comforting, supportive: "We're very hopeful. We have a lot of light out now. It'll be easier."

Paula called Nick's mother, Marcia Schuyler, who lived with her daughter, Kristen, two hours south of Tampa, in Fort Myers. Marcia didn't pick up the call. She was in her living room, speaking with Kristen, who had just walked in the door. Marcia would get back to Paula in a little while. They had some catching up to do.

When the call went to voice mail, Paula was relieved. No one ever wants to tell a mother that her son didn't come home.

Next, Paula tried Kristen Schuyler. This was odd, Kristen thought. It was not like Paula to call that early.

"What's wrong?" Kristen asked.

"It's your brother," Paula said.

Kristen thought they had had a fight or had broken up.

"He's missing," Paula said.

Kristen felt dread in the pit of her stomach. She had driven home earlier in the morning from Tampa, where she had attended a black-tie fund-raiser for breast cancer the night before. She had texted Nick on Saturday night, telling him that Major League baseball players had been in attendance. He had not replied, but this didn't alarm Kristen—Nick sometimes didn't respond unless Kristen asked him a direct question. She had called her brother again this morning to tell Nick about her 5K race on Saturday. Her call went straight to voice mail. Now she knew why. Nick had not returned from his fishing trip. And now the weather had turned cold and windy. This could not be good. The Coast Guard was about to make an announcement on television.

Kristen hung up with Paula, paced around her bedroom and then walked outside without speaking to her mother. She kept waiting for her phone to ring again to say that everything was okay, that Nick was safe and sound. The call didn't come. Ten minutes later, Kristen returned and sat next to her mother in the living room.

"Is everything okay?" Marcia Schuyler asked.

"I don't know," Kristen said.

Marcia noticed a blank look on her daughter's face, as if she had been crying.

"Oh my God, what happened to your brother?" Marcia said.

Nick had not returned home from a fishing trip, Kristen said. Marcia went to the bathroom and threw up. They tossed some clothes into a bag, took a shower, and headed to Tampa. Kristen could hear her mother sobbing in the shower.

She called her father, Stu Schuyler, and he became upset. He had phoned Nick the morning before, telling him the weather was expected to get bad and to come home early.

"Damn it, I told him not to go out," Stu said to his daughter. He was angry, yelling.

"Dad, this is not the time," Kristen said. "This is not going to help."

Kristen was usually the rock of the family. She didn't cry until she got into the shower. Something is really, really wrong, she thought to herself.

Paula Oliveira called Bob and Betty Bleakley, Will's parents. The boys never made it back and the Coast Guard was looking for them. Betty replied that she had told Will the trip was a bad idea. Paula told her the Coast Guard had offered reassuring words. The search would be easier in the daylight.

Within a half hour, Stu Schuyler called Paula. She tried to reassure him, but he was pessimistic. "I'm not oblivious to what Mother Nature can do," Stu said.

"We can't think that way," Paula replied. "We have to stick together and be positive."

"You're right," Stu said.

The storm began to settle down in midmorning or late morning, the waves changing from chop to swells. They were less random, less crazy. Then we began seeing helicopters. You would hear them, then you would see them. They were all in the distance. We would see one, then fifteen minutes later we would see another. Then we didn't see another one for an hour or two. We couldn't tell if it was the same helicopter or not. It didn't really matter. The helicopters were orange and white. We knew they were Coast Guard. We knew they were looking for us.

We would see a helicopter and all of our attention would go to that. We would yell and wave our orange life jackets. We wouldn't pay attention to the waves, and the next thing we knew, a swell would hit us from behind and flip us back into the water.

The helicopters never came real close. It seemed like they were a mile away or more. They seemed higher than the one I thought I saw the night before.

"Help, help, we're down here!" we would scream. I tried to picture what they were looking at, and I had the same thought as last night: our boat would look like just another whitecap among thousands of white waves.

We would see a helicopter and get ready to take our life jackets off and wave them, excited, saying to each other, "Here we go—this is it—this is our chance—they got us!"

"You see one over there?" Will would say, and our hopes would go up, then deflate again. We'd get excited and then frustrated. It didn't feel hopeless, but I felt I was not in control whatsoever. The effort Will and I were putting out was helping us to survive, but not to get rescued. It was like a roller coaster. Help was so near, and then it was gone again.

We kept asking each other, "What else can we do?" We knew our chances were getting smaller and smaller. We were still somewhat hopeful, but not as excited. It was getting further and further along. They had missed us so many times before. I kept thinking about Marquis and Corey, worried that Will and I would begin to deteriorate, too.

"I can't believe they can't see us!" I would yell.

"How can they not see us?!" Will would scream.

He thought about the flares that had been useless the night before.

"I sure wish we had them now," he said. "With those flares, we would have been saved."

AT ABOUT TEN thirty or eleven in the morning, I looked just off the right side of the boat and said, "What the hell is that?"

At first I thought it was a white cloud in the water. But it moved closer and went under the boat. I think it was a squid. It had long, white, purplish-grayish tentacles. They were long and skinny, like a giant version of what we had used for bait the day before. Altogether, it seemed ten feet long. I couldn't see its body, but I could see the tentacles hanging out from under the boat.

Will looked, too.

"Oh my God."

After all we had just gone through in the last twenty-four-plus hours, what could possibly make me more scared than I already was? This was just something else to freak me out. It wasn't moving, it was just floating. The tentacles looked like the alien in *Independence Day,* when Will Smith is dragging it on the ground. Not snakelike, but wet, yolky leather. It was disturbing even to look at.

"No way in hell I'm falling off this boat now," I said.

I didn't know that stuff was in the Gulf. I knew they were in deep water. I knew that when we were fishing the water was 150 feet deep, but here I had no idea: 200-plus feet? 75 feet? I figured it was deep, because I knew the deeper the water, the bigger the waves.

"How do they eat?" I asked Will. "Can they kill us?"

"I think they have beaks," he said.

"Do they sting like jellyfish?" I wanted to know.

It must have stayed under the boat two hours. We bear-hugged each other on the motor, but we did fall off a few times. The squid was behind us, more toward the front of the boat. It was freaky. I would fall in and get right back up. Before, we would sometimes sit in the water to regroup. Now I was scrambling to get right back on the boat. If Will lingered in the water, I would scream at him, "What are you doing? Get out of there!"

At one point, it came within about five feet of us.

"What can it possibly be doing under there?" I asked Will. "Is it getting the fish we caught? Our bait? Is it in the cooler? Is it waiting for us to fall in?"

Sometimes we wouldn't see it. We thought it was gone and then it would come back again.

"I can't believe that thing is still here," I said.

The waves were still kicking. A little less than fifteen feet, about thirteen. The random stuff was gone. They were consistent swells now. And, finally, the squid was gone, too. We never saw it again.

* * *

ONCE WE WERE sure it was no longer beneath the boat, Will took off his life jacket and dived under, looking for cell phones, food— anything that might help us. I told him to be careful. We were bleeding a lot. He would hold on as best he could, wait until the waves were right, take a deep breath, and dive under the boat. Sometimes he judged the wave wrong, got nailed, and came right back up, his mouth full of water. Then he made it under and opened the storage bin, now above the steering wheel. He came up holding my backpack, which contained our cell phones and a pair of my sandals.

I grabbed Will's cell phone, but it was waterlogged and didn't work. I had a water-resistant and shock-resistant phone, a construction type, because I had been through so many of them. I thought it had zero chance of working, but it turned on right away.

Here's another shot, I thought to myself. I got no reception bars, but I dialed 9-1-1 anyway. CONNECTING, it read. CONNECTING and dot, dot, dot. Same as before.

"I don't fucking get it," I said. So much for 9-1-1. A little bit of hope had been shot right back down again.

I sent out a text to Paula, my mother, and my sister: "We're alive, find us."

NO SERVICE. SEND WHEN SERVICE AVAILABLE? it said. I clicked YES.

I would put it away and try again a few minutes later. Still no service. Nothing.

THE NIKE BACKPACK was black, a LeBron James model, L23. He and I were the same age, from the same state. He was from Akron, I was from Chardon. In high school, he was first team All-State; I was third team. We had that in common. We both graduated in

2003. I didn't so much look up to him as keep watch on him. Just small talk, like, "You see what LeBron put up last night?" Every week, they would run the scoring averages of the top players in the state, and he would be near the top or at the top, and I would be in the middle of the list somewhere. You always saw his name on TV and in the paper. He was on the cover of *Sports Illustrated*. It was cool because he was an hour away. I remember one big newspaper article, a whole page, and it had some of his features. He was 6 feet 7 inches, 220 or 230, with freak-of-nature speed, strong hands, a muscular build. I knew he was awesome. They talked about him being the next Michael Jordan. He was good in football, too. He was like an All-State receiver as a sophomore. We wanted to play them, but it never worked out.

When he got drafted by the Cavaliers, I became a big fan. He's a humble guy. His idol was his mother. We were alike in that way, too. She worked extra hours or extra jobs just to make sure food was on the table. His mother was his best friend. She always put him first. She never missed a game. She reminded me of my mom.

THE BOAT SEEMED a little lower in the water, and we kept wondering whether there was anything we could use for flotation if it eventually sank. I remembered the week before, when Corey asked Marquis if he had any life jackets on the boat. "Yeah, we got life jackets," Marquis had said. "This entire boat is a life jacket."

The sides of the boat were cushioned. You could lean your thighs against the sides when you fished. It wasn't soft like a pillow, but it was soft leather. Marquis also said the cushions came off the two seats in the back of the boat. Will went under again, but came up empty-handed.

"It's not coming off," he said.

He tried a second time, and after he seemed to be under a good ten seconds, he kind of ripped off one of the seat cushions. He swam to the back of the boat and handed it to me. The cushion had little grooved panels on it.

"This'll work," I said.

Will seemed exhausted. He had been holding his breath, fighting the waves and the current to get under the boat. He seemed to use all his strength to get that cushion loose. When he came up, I could hear him gasping for breath. It was like he was seconds away from drowning or had run a bunch of sprints. He was spitting water from his mouth. We hadn't talked about taking turns under the boat. He was the better swimmer, and he had been under the day before, so he knew what everything looked like.

I found an immediate use for the cushion. I put it between my crotch and the motor. I would take a hit from a wave and slam forward, and there was almost no pain. It was like having a protective cup in football. When I smashed up against the engine, at least now it was tolerable.

"God, that's so much better," I told Will. He was so amazing to think of others ahead of himself.

IN EARLY AFTERNOON, a giant Coast Guard plane flew directly over us. It was orange and white and seemed bigger and fatter than a 747. And it seemed to be flying slow. It came from behind us and it seemed so close that I could almost throw a baseball that high. If I had a flare, I felt like I would have hit the plane.

We swung our life jackets again. We knew the plane couldn't stop like a helicopter and hover. We knew that it wouldn't drop anything for us. But we were excited: "We got it, we got it!" we hollered. "They found us! This is it!"

We yelled, "Thank you, God!" We were just hoping they had marked our exact location, our precise longitude and latitude. We knew they saw us. Or we hoped they did. Surely, they would send someone back to pick us up. Then we saw nothing for probably two hours. That was a complete buzzkill. Here was our chance to get out of it. Two out of four of us, anyway. And now, nothing.

"They had to see us," I said to Will. "There's no way they couldn't see us."

The plane had flown straight for a long distance. It didn't change directions. Maybe the pilots were distracted at that particular moment they flew over us, I thought grimly. Maybe one of the Coast Guards was going to the bathroom or not looking down. They'll probably head back to shore now to refuel, I thought. I was pissed.

We had been in the water almost twenty-four hours. At this point, we were both feeling defenseless, feeling like we were just waiting to die. Neither of us said it out loud, but we both felt like there was nothing more for us to do. We really just had to sit there and wait.

"Please, God," I said. "I'll do anything. Please, God."

A while later, as we crested a wave, Will said, "Is that land over there?"

We went back and forth.

"I don't know," I said.

We kept talking. We had been awake for almost thirty-six hours. We were cold and starving. Were we hallucinating, too?

"I don't know if I'm frickin' losing it or what," I said to Will.

"Dude," he said. "I think that's land."

It was about midafternoon. We kept looking, trying to convince ourselves that we weren't imagining this. We went back and forth for ten minutes. We rode up one wave, then another, trying to stand slightly off the hull to get a view from higher up. It looked like some taller buildings, maybe off of a beach. They appeared to be seven or eight miles away. They were tall, rectangular buildings, or almost like big drums or a water tower. Cylinder-shaped.

The Coast Guard would later say that it was highly unlikely that we saw land. Maybe it was a passing freighter or cargo ship. At that moment, though, desperate for hope, after ten minutes of going back and forth, we decided it was land. Now, what were we going to do about it?

"Dude, do we take a chance on it?" Will said.

"I don't know," I said. "I don't know how far that is."

"Well, it's at least five miles," he said. "If we're drifting toward that way, if we can swim a couple miles per hour, we'll be there before it's dark."

I wasn't concerned that Will was too tired after diving under the boat again. He was a terrific swimmer. And we were desperate.

For another half hour we debated whether to swim for it. We hadn't seen a plane in a while. The sun never really poked out. If we stayed with the boat, maybe things would get worse than they already were. The waves were straight swells, one after another. We were able to stay on the boat for the most part. Every twenty minutes or so, a random wave would come and knock us off. But it was much better than before.

Finally, Will said, "What do you think?"

"I don't know," I said.

I asked again about sharks.

"Do you think sharks can get us?" I asked Will.

"I don't think so, no," he said.

I knew there were sharks out there. We had caught some on our trip. Small ones, but they were still sharks.

I asked him about the blood from our legs. We were bleeding from being tossed around so much and banging ourselves on the motor. I could see blood on the boat. Will only had his swimsuit on and a T-shirt under his life jacket. His legs were bleeding. I knew it was a possibility that could attract sharks. You always hear about that stuff.

"It's too rough," Will said. "They're not going to come up this high."

That made sense. I dropped it from my mind.

But there was something else to worry about. If we tried to swim, how would we stay together in the water?

I got an idea. There was a black wire connected to the motor. The steering cable, I guessed. I thought it connected to the helm. I started pulling it. It took all my strength, but I yanked it through the keel six inches at a time and tore one end free. Then I cut the other end off, slicing it on the propeller. It had lots of little wires inside. It seemed similar to the wire used for cable TV.

The cable was stiff. You could tie a knot, but it wasn't very tight. The wire was probably ten feet long, about as thick as a pen or a pretzel rod.

We could tie the cable between us, I told Will.

"That way we won't lose each other," I said.

We decided to make a run for it.

I tied one end of the wire to my life jacket, and Will tied the other end to his. We kind of slid into the water and started to go. I grabbed the cushion that was shielding me from the motor and asked Will, "Do I bring this thing?"

Sure, he said. I tried it under my stomach for a few minutes, riding it like a Boogie board, but it wasn't buoyant enough. Waves would hit me from behind and I would go under. Or I couldn't hold my head up.

"Should I get rid of this?" I asked.

"I don't know," Will said. "It's up to you."

I didn't really have a choice. It was holding me back. I couldn't hold it, swim, and kick at the same time. I let go of the cushion and it slowly floated away. We kind of floated on our backs in our life jackets, but I was still feeling sluggish.

We were pretty close to each other, about five feet, kind of kicking, but not moving at all. We would go all the way up the wave and all the way back down, but we weren't going forward.

"Hold on a sec," I said.

My sneakers were weighing me down. I took them off. They were Nike Shoxx, with copper-colored heels. The week before, I had worn my good sneakers on Marquis's boat, but we hauled up so many fish on deck, my shoes got all bloody. I was pissed. I had just gotten them the month before for my birthday. I got the stains out, but I wasn't risking it again. This time, I wore an old pair. I kind of leaned back in the water and took one shoe off, then the other. One floated on top for a few moments, the other hovered just under the surface.

I took off my sweatpants, too. That was a mistake. Immediately I felt colder. I still had my orange winter jacket and sweatshirt on, but all I had on my legs now were my swim trunks. They were bright yellow, with a tropical print, a white-and-yellow flower.

In the open water, it was impossible to judge whether we were making any leeway. It didn't seem so. We continued to swim on our backs for a good five or ten minutes, but we weren't more than fifty yards from the boat. We weren't moving closer to anything, especially to the land I couldn't see anymore, or what we thought was land.

"Will, this isn't working," I said, frustrated.

"No, it's not," Will said.

I was hoping we could almost ride the waves toward shore, but the current seemed to be pulling us farther out to sea. The boat was kind of following us. We were big guys, and the life jackets weren't holding us up real well. They were rising up, almost choking us. It was uncomfortable. And the steering wire wasn't working, either. If we got more than a few feet from each other, one guy would get pulled back or ripped down or his life jacket would get yanked up.

"What do you think we should do?" I asked Will.

"I don't know," he said.

Neither one of us wanted to abandon the plan, but we didn't have much of a choice.

"We need to go back to the boat," I said.

"Okay."

It took us a good ten minutes or so to get back to the boat. We kicked and kicked but hardly seemed to move. Eventually, finally, we climbed back onto the hull. We were exhausted and mad. We had just had the worst swim ever, and now I didn't have my shoes or sweatpants. I was barefoot. My feet were white and pruned. With no shoes, I had to watch were I was stepping now. Trying to climb back onto the boat, I cut my foot on a piece of metal. I grabbed my sandals from my backpack and put them on.

I looked at the inside of my legs. They were brittle and had gashes. Blood was dripping down. Everything on my legs felt like an exposed nerve. All my bones hurt. My knees were killing me. My shins were bad, my ankles were bad. My lower back was shot. My right hip still hurt so bad from holding Marquis. I could use it, but I knew something was wrong.

We thought we had a good opportunity by swimming for it. We didn't want to sit there and wait and die on that boat. We weren't going to give up, even if we had to swim ten miles to get discovered. But in that amount of water, with those waves, you can get turned around real quick. I got in place next to the motor and for a few minutes, I didn't think about the cushion that I had let float away. Then a wave nailed us, and my crotch took another hit. I was in excruciating pain and thought, Why did I let that cushion go? For what?

Will bear-hugged me from behind. It was midafternoon. I could feel him shaking.

Three cutters had been docked at the St. Petersburg Coast Guard station. Not all were operational. The *Hawk*'s engines were stripped down in the middle of a scheduled maintenance period. The *Alligator* was still being outfitted and had not yet been commissioned. The *Crocodile,* an eighty-seven-foot coastal patrol boat, was dispatched early on Sunday morning, but it had no more luck finding the missing Everglades boat than did the motor lifeboat, the C-130s, and the Jayhawk helicopters.

"It was a lousy ride" in whitecapped seas that reached fourteen feet, Captain Timothy Close, commander of the St. Petersburg Coast Guard station, said of the *Crocodile*. "By the end of the day on Sunday, the senior officer said, 'We're good for a two-hundred-yard-wide swath. Beyond that we're not effective. You can't really see anything.' We were like, 'You're done. Come back in.'"

All told, the Coast Guard would have two hundred personnel involved in forty-eight separate search patterns for the missing boaters by planes, jets, helicopters, and ships. No more than a period of twenty minutes passed without someone actively searching, Captain Close said. Eventually, the searches would total 24,000 square miles. Many of the searches were overlapping tracks that concentrated on a grid 60 miles offshore and 100 miles north and south of the original spot where the boaters were believed to have gone fishing.

At one thirty on Sunday afternoon, Captain Close had called his boss in Miami and said, "The weather's bad; I need a bigger cutter."

The *Tornado,* a 179-foot cutter, was patrolling the Florida Straits between Key West and Cuba. Its normal mission was to disrupt illegal immigration and drug trafficking. Since it was already under way, the *Tornado* could get north to Tampa faster than a cutter that was tied up in Key West and might be thirty hours from reaching the search area.

"We weren't going to send the motor lifeboat out again," Captain Close said. "It was terrible weather. We needed larger stuff."

As Marcia and Kristen Schuyler traveled toward St. Petersburg from Fort Myers, they crossed the enormous Sunshine Skyway Bridge that stands more than four hundred feet tall and traverses Tampa Bay. Usually, the view was spectacular for miles, but it had begun to rain and there were whitecaps in the bay.

"Oh my God, look at those waves," Marcia Schuyler said to her daughter, who had begun to get extremely scared. Through the afternoon, Marcia kept crying and saying, "I can't lose your brother."

They arrived at the Coast Guard station in St.

Petersburg and spoke with Captain Close. The station was right on the water, a white stucco building with a Spanish-tiled roof. The building was built in a way that made it seem hunkered down against a storm. Captain Close was cordial and supportive. He showed them the command center and told the Schuylers that everything possible was being done to find their son and his friends. The Schuylers left their phone numbers. Captain Close told them to call anytime.

Marcia and Kristen left the station about three thirty, avoiding the news media parked outside. Stu Schuyler, Nick's father, arrived, and he was upset.

"It's not good," he said to Kristen. "I know he's gone."

"Don't you dare say that," Kristen replied.

Her father was inconsolable.

"I'll kill myself if he's gone," Stu said to Kristen. "I can't live without him."

Stu Schuyler walked to a pier at the Coast Guard station and was told by someone that the forty-seven-foot motor lifeboat sent out earlier that morning had returned. Rough seas had hampered the search for the missing boaters.

Stu thought to himself that if his Jet Ski wasn't under repair, he would ride into the Gulf to help the rescue attempt. He knew it was a foolish idea, but his son was out there. Anything was better than standing around. How he and his ex-wife didn't have heart attacks he couldn't explain. Stu and his second wife, Jackie, spoke briefly to the media, believing it might somehow help in the search. At least it couldn't hurt, though it was hardly comforting.

Stu kept saying to himself, They're in the water. I know they're in the water.

A short while after we swam back to the boat, Will said he was thirsty.

"There's got to be more stuff under the boat," he said.

Earlier, he had wondered, "You think we can eat some of that fish we caught yesterday?"

On the floor of the boat, in the back, was a trapdoor that folded back. It was the box where we kept the fish. It was a production every time we caught one. We had five plastic gasoline cans back there. We had to move them to open the door and toss the fish in.

As I said, I hate fish, the taste, the smell, the texture, everything, except for maybe that time Marquis forced me to have a bit of the grilled and fried fish after our first fishing trip. It probably started when I was nine or ten, and my mom tricked me at Long John Silver's. She told me it was chicken until I ate most of what was on my plate. Then she said, "You just ate fish." I was so mad, I spit out what was in my mouth and threw down the piece I had in my hand. But now I was hungry. I would have contemplated eating my own arm.

This fish wasn't cooked, though. It might not even be dead.

"Would we get sick on it?" I asked Will.

"Well, there's sushi," he said. "People eat sushi and don't get sick."

I thought about how disgusting it would be, holding a fifteen-pound fish and gnawing on something that might still be alive. But I was willing to do it if it worked. Still, I had another concern and I brought it up with Will: "If we open that fish box and there was no water in there, is it going to take on water and is the boat going to go down?"

We went back and forth, and finally decided not to take a chance.

If the boat went down, we were both screwed. Still, we were starving.

"I'm going to try to go back under," Will said.

Will had ripped free one of the twenty-gallon coolers the day before. There was one remaining. The cooler was wedged in place between the deck and the captain's chair at the center console. Before we set out, Marquis had secured the lid tightly with a bungee cord. Now the whole thing would be upside down.

"There's got to be some sandwiches," I said.

We were so thirsty and hungry. We had given everything to Marquis at his house, and he had stored it on the boat. We knew he hadn't put a couple of cases of beer in the coolers. But we didn't know if the beer had fallen off the boat when we turned over. We figured there was more stuff in the storage bin where Will had found the backpack. It was like a small closet.

He went under a few times and got nothing. He came up gasping for air. It had only been a few seconds, but it seemed like he had been holding his breath for minutes. I got nervous. Suppose he hit his head and didn't come back up?

He came up another time and said, "I think I can get to the cooler."

"The sandwiches have got to be in there," I said.

"I'll reach in and grab what I can," he said.

With the bungee cord holding the lid shut and the waves moving the boat, he would only have a few seconds. He went under twice more, and then the third time, he brought up a bottle of Gatorade. G2, low-calorie. Twenty ounces. Purple—my least favorite, but beggars can't be choosers. I held on to it. I didn't drink it right away.

"I think I can get some more," Will said.

He went back down two more times and got nothing.

"I'm gonna try once more," he said.

It was exhausting him. I could see it in his eyes. I could hear him breathing hard. He looked very pale, very tired. Still, he went under again and the third time, and he was able to retrieve a small bag of pretzels. Pretzel bits, I think they were called. Little squares. They were honey-mustard. Usually, I would have eaten fish before I ate those pretzels. But at this point, I was happy with anything. And I was grateful to have Will with me. He was beating himself up, going under the boat. Still, I never thought the two of us wouldn't get out of it. We had already fought those waves earlier in the day, and now they weren't so choppy; we were able to stay out of the water for the most part.

We split the Gatorade. We took real little sips. I drank exactly half. It was almost like a tease. My throat was hurting so bad, like real bad strep throat. It almost felt like my throat was cracking. It didn't do a lot of good.

"Do you like it?" Will asked.

"Yeah, sweet," I said. It seemed like I tasted every single flavor in the drink.

The pretzels were so dry. Will took a couple, but that was it.

"I can't eat those," he said.

"Why'd you buy this nasty shit?" I had asked Will the night before our trip.

They were all we had now, and they were better than nothing, but they were as dry as dirt.

"Dude, you should try them," I said.

"No, I can't," he said.

I was so hungry, I ate as many as I could. I don't know if I was eating too fast or not swallowing all the way, but the pretzels were getting stuck in my throat. My mouth and throat felt blistered. I was choking the food down.

I tried to keep the bag closed to keep the water out. We only had a quarter of a bag left when a wave landed on us. The pretzels went from damp to soaked.

"You want any more?" I asked. "They're done."

"No," he said, and I let them go.

WILL WENT BACK under a couple times. He was a man on a mission, but he wasn't able to pull anything up. He was physically drained now—he had nothing left. Getting back on the boat was like trying to climb a fence. If you didn't give it everything, you weren't going to do it. Will floated in the water for a while and said, "I'm so tired. My heart is beating so fast."

Sometimes he stayed in the water five minutes or more, hanging on to a trim tab. I had to help him back on the boat. He sat behind me, holding on. It was quiet. We worked together as best we could, leaning into the waves. Sometimes, we still got thrown into the water. Will was now falling in a lot more than I did. We were both tired, but he had the added toll of diving under the boat so many times. We both put up with the same repetitive thing, hour after hour. Sit. Fall. Climb on. Sit. Fall. Climb on. Sometimes, for nine or ten minutes, I'd sit there in the water, too, holding on to the swim platform or a trim tab, and I'd just float.

Please God, I prayed. I'll do anything.

I thought similar thoughts that I had the day before. It was probably after three or four in the afternoon. We were physically exhausted. All we could do was wait and wait. And hope. I just wanted to let my mother know that I was still alive, that I was okay. I didn't want her to worry, or at least I wanted her to worry less. I wanted the Coast Guard to continue to look for us and for her to know I was alive.

I knew how my mom got. I knew how me and my sister had always come first and how my mom went out of her way to make our day better even if it made her day worse. I knew everyone was worried and scared. We were scared, too, but I wanted them to know that we were fighting, and as long as they were looking, we would keep fighting.

Will and I said the Lord's Prayer again as I held the cross on my necklace.

"Please, God, I'll start going to church every Sunday," I said.

We hadn't seen a plane or a helicopter in a while.

"I can't believe they can't find us," Will said a few times.

When the choppers had come and gone, Will had cried out in sheer frustration, rage, and disappointment. We felt helpless and discouraged. We were busting our asses, working so hard to survive.

Once, Will was in the water and he peed, and he said, "Oh my God." It felt so good. I wondered how he could pee when he was so dehydrated. I said, "Why didn't you wait until I was in the water so I could feel the warmth?"

I had no idea where we were. We could have been close to the Bahamas or to Cuba. We could have been a mile from where we overturned or close to Texas. I had no clue. I felt helpless. I didn't know what we were going to do the next minute but sit there and pray and hope. We were always looking for a buoy. At least it would be stationary. We could cling to it. But there were no buoys out here.

My legs were bleeding real bad. The salt water made the cuts a lot worse. I was in a lot of pain. My ass was torn up from sitting on the keel. A wave would come from the front of the boat and shoot up my back. It took my breath away. I had that same taste in my mouth, almost like crystal, like I was tasting my teeth.

I put salt water in my mouth and rinsed it around and spit it out just to have some kind of moisture. I thought my body had already burned all its fat, most of it in my butt, and now I felt it was burning muscle. I was losing whatever padding I had, and it was getting more painful to sit on the keel.

I thought about a million things. About life, about people who really mattered. I wondered what I would do if I got out of this. What would I do differently now that I had had a reality check? How would my life change? Will's life?

I thought about what had happened with Marquis and Corey the night before. How would I explain it if we got rescued? Particularly to their families. How would I explain that Will and I made it while we lost both of them? Why did the NFL players die and the two best friends live? Why did two white kids live and two black guys die? Would someone try to make a racial incident out of it? Crazy thoughts.

I kept thinking about how I had to let go of Marquis, his head flopped back, his lifeless body floating in the water. His eyes were closed. I thought how that was the last time anyone would see him. I was the last one to say anything to him. I thought about holding on to his wrist, and finally letting go. Over and over.

I went through the whole thing in my mind. Why is this happening to me? I wondered. Is this karma for things I've done bad in my life?

I asked God, "Please."

I thought about high school, about friends who had grown distant and apart. I thought about my couple of years at college at

Kent State. They were probably the best two years of my life, meeting new friends, staying up late, playing video games when I should have been studying and sleeping, eating crap food and going out late and partying. I thought about how I moved to Florida, wanting something different, a new start. I was over living in dorms and ugly, rainy weather.

I thought about working out a lot and my best friend at home, Nate Milstead. He went to Kent with me. We lived on the same floor of the same dorm. He got hurt in a snowboarding accident, damaging his back and rupturing his spleen. His family was in a tough financial situation, so he had to leave school. He went into the army. He was so frightened he would get deployed to Iraq. The last time he visited me in Florida, he was scared to death. He believed he wasn't going to come back. He had too much to drink one night down here and got all emotional. He said to tell his little brother Zack that he loved him. "Tell my mother I love her," he said. "I'm not stupid. I know I'm not coming back."

But his back was so messed up, he got out of the army. He was excited, ecstatic. He became a cop in Akron. That's what he wanted to be. He was a hands-on guy, good with people. But that night down here he had been so scared. And now I was as scared as he was.

I thought again about all the important people in my life. My high school girlfriend, Megan Frank. She was married now. I thought back to the motorcycle accident with my friend Daniel Turner. I thought about my friend from college, Matt Smith, who has muscular dystrophy, and how fortunate I was. I thought about another friend, Ryan Barry, and how we partied at school and joked around. I thought about Amanda Smith, a girl I had partied with in high school.

I thought again about how worried my mother surely was, and

that she was doing all she could do, and the Coast Guard was sending choppers and everyone was doing as much as possible, but I knew people felt helpless as well, as helpless as I did.

I thought about how I couldn't have my mother come to my funeral. I knew if I didn't make it through this, my mom was going to have to go through life without her son. That's probably the worst thing a mother can go through, losing a child. A parent shouldn't have to bury a child. It should be the other way around. No one is strong enough for that.

I could picture my mother making the arrangements with the church and the funeral home and the graveyard. I tried not to think about it, but I couldn't help it. I thought about who would attend my funeral. I went through everybody in my head, friends, aunts, uncles, cousins, the parents of my friends. Even my old teachers and coaches. Would they come all the way down from up north? It made me extremely sad.

I thought about one of my favorite teachers, my third-grade teacher, Mrs. Sweet. I felt like I was her favorite student. She was a short and cute older woman who found a way to make everything funny and not school-like. She'd read stories to the class. She changed voices for each character. If there were five characters, she changed voices for each one.

Third grade was still my favorite grade. Nine years old. Carefree. When we had show-and-tell, the one who gave the presentation would leave the class and everyone would comment and say good things about that person. We all had a chart and she would laminate comments on it. One of the kids had commented about me, "He's cute."

Third grade was my first year of football. The Munson Mustangs. We went to the Pee Wee Super Bowl. I was one of the fastest guys in the league. Some of the parents called me a ball hog and gave me a hard time, even though the coaches called the plays. I scored fourteen touchdowns that year. We lost in the championship game, six to nothing. I had never cried about sports, but after that game, I broke down. It was the only game I hadn't scored. I felt like it was my fault.

I thought about my sports career beyond that. I think every athlete has this characteristic, whether they admit it or not: "When I'm in my prime I can do it, I can go another step." Like I had the night before, I thought back to some decisions I made—not continuing to play football my last two years of high school. I knew I had a better chance in college with football than basketball. I thought about how I had torn my ACL the summer after my senior year of high school—hurt it in a pickup game. I thought about working out with Marquis and Corey and how I was in just as good a shape as both of them. I had done endurance lifting for so long, and it was new to them. Constantly moving, resting one body part while working another, ninety minutes to two hours of constant work.

I thought about my chances to play football at USF. What if I had stuck it out and sat out one year and played the next? Another year—you think that's a long time, but it's really not. I should have stuck it out.

Everything in my mind now was what-ifs. What if I don't make it out of here? What if that plane did see us and is making its way back? What if no one finds us? There was a lot of hope and prayer and frustration.

IT WAS PROBABLY five o'clock at this point. We had seen maybe one more helicopter in the distance. I took my life jacket off and swung it over my head, but nothing. The chopper flew away. The sky was kind of overcast. Earlier in the day the sun would poke out for ten or fifteen seconds once in a while. It was so nice. "I wish it would stay out," Will and I kept saying. Then the sun would go behind a cloud. You could really feel the difference.

The swells, consistent ten-footers, were getting a little more choppy. We were still getting thrown off the boat. There were no big gusts of wind like before, but we were still freezing. I looked at my legs. There were little cuts all over, particularly on my calves. My butt was bleeding. I could see blood on the back of my knees. My ass and my back hurt so bad. My knees were scraped up, and pieces of skin were missing. The strawberries you get on your hip from sliding into home plate, I had them all over my body. I felt contusions and bone bruises. My hands were freezing. I still had my gloves, but the fingers were shredded. It felt like my fingers were broken.

I had the sandals from my backpack, but the tops of my feet were getting torn up, holding on against a trim tab or the swim platform, gashing my feet against metal and fiberglass. Will's arms and legs were cut up pretty bad, too. My neck was stiff. It felt like someone had taken a baseball bat and swung at me. I was completely slouched over, sitting on the keel, my shoulders forward, just holding on to that motor for dear life. I tried to burrow myself into my jacket, to get my chin under my sweatshirt so that only my eyes showed.

Will and I were getting quieter and quieter. I could tell he was getting weak. We would get thrown into the water and it would take him longer and longer to get back on the boat. Or he would just float for a while, out of energy. "Oh my God, I'm so cold," he said. He was choked-up, sad.

"Don't worry," I told him. "They're gonna find us."

I helped him get back on, and we prayed and hoped some more.

By now, he had gone off the boat quite a few times. He was sitting behind me on the hull, still trying to bear-hug me, but I was getting limited effort from him, almost zero effort. Earlier, when a wave would come, he would balance himself and work with me. Now, he was ripping me down into the water with him. He must have pulled me in six or seven times.

He was very, very weak. I knew he was exhausted from going under the boat as much as he did.

"You all right?" I kept asking him through the day.

"Yeah," he would say.

Now his answers were getting weaker. I'd have to call his name a couple times before he replied.

Whatever was going on was bad. Will was sluggish. His strength was going. He looked tired, he squinted his eyes. He kept saying, "I'm so cold, I'm so thirsty."

"Will, you gotta hold on," I told him.

He kept asking what time it was. We hadn't seen any helicopters for a while. I knew dusk was coming quick. It was getting colder out. I could feel it. The temperature in the air was cold. It would end up being one of the coldest nights of the year, in the sixties or the high fifties. All Will had on was a T-shirt, his swim trunks, and his life jacket. I remembered what he had said earlier in the day, "I'll never make it through another night." This was probably the most scared I had been.

Then we started seeing fins. The first was a gray rectangle sticking out of the water, probably eight feet from the boat. I didn't say anything right away. All of a sudden I was really alert. Twenty seconds later, I saw the fin again, so I wasn't hallucinating. It wasn't a dolphin. I knew they kind of rolled through the water, slanting up and down. This was swimming more in a straight line. The fin would come up for a few seconds. You'd see a little more fin, a little more, then less and then it was gone.

"Will, you have to stay on the boat," I said to him. "I think there are sharks."

There were two of them. I don't think they were anything large, maybe five-footers. They looked similar to the lemon sharks we had caught on Saturday, but I couldn't tell for sure. I assumed the blood leaking off the boat had attracted them. Or the bait under the boat. We had so much bait loose when it flipped. I knew sharks didn't usually come up unless there was food.

I had gone scuba diving a couple times in St. Thomas and outside Cancun. At first, I was scared. Am I really going down here? Then I thought it would be kind of cool to see a shark. But that was on vacation, not when I was stranded in the Gulf, defenseless and bloody. I never liked being in open water, even when I was a kid and we went tubing and I fell off. My dad had a boat. We'd go tubing in a river or along the coast. I had a phobia about sharks. I'd rather have taken my chances with a gator.

I saw the fins five times in probably a ten-minute span. A wave would come, and Will and I would slide all the way to the side, like we were about to lose our grip, then I would rip us back up. I was working for both of us.

"Just hold on to me," I told him.

I thought about how I would lift my feet up if the sharks came near the motor. Our blood was dripping there.

It was hard staying on the boat. I knew putting Will in front, on the motor, wouldn't work. He couldn't have held on for both of us, and I would crush him if a wave hit us from behind. He was holding on some, trying to bear-hug me, but there were times when we almost started falling off. I would flip us back upright.

Good thing I work out, I said to myself.

I was aware of the cold, but I was more worried about Will. I thought what Marquis had said on Saturday, that sharks would probably be scared of this white boat above them. They might think it was some kind of animal.

Earlier on Sunday, thinking about what might be swimming beneath us, I said to Will, "Do you know how much shit is looking at us in this water?"

And then the sharks were gone. Like the squid, they just went away. As it turned out, the fear and anticipation had been worse than the reality of seeing one.

The next hour after that, we must have gone off the boat fifteen times. Another twenty times, I yanked Will back before we fell in. I continued pumping my chest, trying to keep the blood flowing. I could feel Will shivering. His teeth were chattering. You could hear the trembling in his voice. It was almost like an echo: "I'm so cooold," and "Why can't they fiiind us?" and "Pleeease, God."

IT WAS GETTING to be late afternoon. We had seen only that one plane and that final helicopter. "Where are the boats?" I asked Will.

I was extremely worried. I could see Will's eyes, the frightened look on his face. It was like the first little sign when someone is going to cry, that look, very scared, very weak. Before, he had been hugging me; now he was completely leaning on me with all of his weight. He said a couple more times, "I'm so cold." He was choked up. There was quivering in his words. "I'm so thirsty," he said again.

Will kept falling off the boat more frequently. Every ten minutes, then five minutes, then three, then two. He struggled more than ever to get back on the boat. I had tied the steering cable to his life jacket, but the jacket was slightly torn. Then I tied the cable to his wrist, but it began hurting his hand. So I tied the cable back to his jacket. The other end was tied to the motor. At times, when Will fell into the water, he didn't grab on to anything. He just floated. He would drift eight or ten feet away. Sometimes I jumped off and swam out and brought him back to the boat. Luckily, we had that cable.

"Come on, Will, come on," I yelled at him. "You ain't gonna fucking quit on me."

This went on for half an hour. He was getting beat up. Waves that shouldn't have knocked us off the boat were flipping us in the water. What little strength Will had left, he was losing quickly. He squeezed me from behind, but there didn't seem to be any fight left in him. He had done so much for me, and now he was fading. I couldn't hold on for both of us. Sometimes it was easier for him to drift for a little while in the water, but it was so cold. The waves were getting real choppy again, like they had been twelve hours earlier, before sunrise.

Swells were still there, but mostly they were random waves, ten-footers. The water temperature felt like it was in the low sixties. The air was definitely getting colder, and the wind was picking up again. The sun hadn't been out for a while. Any warmth had vanished.

The boat would rise a little bit and then slam back into the water. We were both torn up. I kept looking down and seeing blood on my legs. My hands were bleeding through the tears in my gloves. Will was bleeding from his legs. You could see it running down the boat.

"You're not leaving," I told Will. "I'm not letting you die."

He was real quiet. He just couldn't get back on the boat. I'll never forget his face, just very frightened, sad, super-pale.

When he did climb back on the boat, he began rambling and mumbling. I couldn't really make out what he was saying. It was Marquis and Corey all over again, but without the aggression. He started slurring randomly, like they had. He spoke in a deeper tone. It seemed like his lips weren't opening or that he was saying his words backward.

"I love you, Will," I told him. I probably said that a dozen times. "Paula loves you, too."

I told him, "You'll always be my best friend. You'll always be Paula's best friend."

The cable attached to his jacket came untied. The wire was ripping back and forth in the waves and it came loose. My hands were cramped and I struggled to tie a tight knot while sitting on the hull.

"Come on, Will, give me something!" I screamed. "Swim, swim! Will, don't give up on me!"

Two of us were gone, but two of us were going to get out of this, I told him. Help was on the way. They would find us soon. I don't know if I believed it. I just said it.

"I'm not going to lose you!" I kept yelling. "You ain't dying on me!" And "I can't do this without you. I need you here. I'm not going to let you go!"

I started getting emotional. I was very frustrated. Once again I felt absolutely helpless. I had already had two guys die, one in my arms. I was in the middle of witnessing my best friend do the same. I knew these could be his final moments. I wasn't crying, but I was upset, trying to hold it together. My brain was going crazy. I was trying to think of a million things I could do for him.

I was begging, "God, please help!"

We had struggled together the entire day. Part of the reason I still had it together was Will. Now there was nothing I could do for him. I knew I wasn't far from being in the same shape he was in.

I kept thinking about everything that had gone wrong. The boat flipped, we were in a storm, the water was freezing. Marquis got sick, Marquis was gone. Corey got sick, Corey was gone. Daylight came, but a storm came with it. We couldn't see, it was pouring, the waves got stronger. Help from the Coast Guard was above us numerous times, then the helicopters were gone. Thank God Will got the life jackets and the food, even if it was little more than a tease. I kept saying, "Something good's going to happen. It can't be all bad. We're gonna get a break."

But the only good thing that happened was the boat stayed afloat and we had each other. There were no breaks.

Will weighed 230 and I was 240, and when I swam out to pull him back in, we would go underwater. The life jackets were dinky. They held you afloat, but not enough to keep you above the crashing waves. I kept bringing Will back to the boat. He was gagging and coughing. He started taking in a lot of salt water. His mouth was opening up. He kept spitting up and coughing, something I had seen before with Marquis.

My heart was racing from swimming. I could barely move my legs, I was so exhausted. For a few minutes, I hadn't thought about being cold. I forgot about being thirsty. My main concern was Will. He hadn't been on the boat for a while. I was wearing my backpack now, over my jacket and my sweatshirt. It was a little cumbersome to swim, but when Will got loose from the steering cable, I had to go after him.

"You gotta hold on, gotta work with me a little bit!" I told him. I was yelling, getting frustrated. As bad as everything was, all that had happened in the last twenty-four hours, it was getting even worse. I was in the midst of losing the last person I had with me. My best friend. He was deteriorating before my eyes.

I kept wondering, Why is he getting so bad, and I'm not?

I guess I knew why. He had a lot less clothing on. He had gone under the boat a bunch of times. I knew that had completely exhausted him.

We attempted to get back on the boat one final time. I got up and straddled the motor and helped Will get up. I was literally using every ounce of strength I had left. I told him, "I love you. I love you so much.".

I was getting upset. "I love you, too," he said. But this time he was real slow, kind of quiet, half crying. That made me even more upset.

I told him, "We're going to be each other's best man at our weddings."

A minute later, Will got tossed back into the water. He came off the side, falling to our left. "Grab on!" I yelled. The steering cable was tied to his jacket and the motor. When he flew into the water, his jacket stayed above the surface as he submerged. I don't know if it got out of whack as he went down or what. It was choking him when his head popped back up. He lifted the jacket off his neck, and it just flew off.

"Will, Will, grab your jacket, no!" I yelled.

He didn't respond.

He was near the boat, and I was straddling the motor. I grabbed him and put his hand on the stern, on the swim platform. I told him to grab his jacket, but he looked at me, delirious. In a few seconds, the jacket was probably thirty feet from the boat. A wave had come by and taken it away. It went from five feet to twenty-five feet in what seemed like a couple seconds.

I tied the cable to his wrist, but it was hard to tie a knot and it kept getting looser and looser. Five minutes later, he kind of wriggled it off. He was confused. He was exhausted, and it was hard for him to swim.

I thought, should I leave Will alone and go and try to get the jacket? Do I wait with him? It was an obvious choice. I couldn't leave him floating there without a life jacket. Within a couple minutes, I couldn't see the jacket anymore. The waves had taken it away.

I had watched my best friend lose all his motor functions in front of me. He could barely talk. I would speak to him and he would just look at me. Earlier, he could tread water, but now his legs were barely kicking. It was a struggle just to hold on. Sometimes one hand would let go of the boat, then the other. It seemed like the waves were getting worse.

It was six o'clock now. I told Will again, "I love you." He answered was slow, quiet. "I love you, too."

His face was droopy, sad. His eyes were shutting. His head was bobbing, almost like he was going to sleep. He was coughing up water.

"Hang on, hang on!" I kept yelling.

I got flipped off the boat. I climbed back on and tried to lift him up with me, but he was deadweight now, no strength at all. I pulled him, but it wasn't going to happen. A series of waves ripped me from the boat again. We were both in the water now. He was a little closer to the boat than I was. We were about ten feet apart. He kind of went underwater. I grabbed him and pulled him up.

"Hold on, Will," I said. "Hold on."

He could barely keep his eyes open. He kept coughing.

"Please God, we need a miracle," I said aloud.

I kept thinking, Why is this happening to us? Why is this happening to him? He's one of best guys I know. I thought about how Marquis and Corey were also some of the best guys I ever met. Why is this happening? I kept asking. There're a lot more evil people in the world than these guys.

Random waves kept crashing into the boat. They were a little smaller but quicker. It was getting choppier. The waves were six to eight feet high, but they were more frequent, a lot rougher. We would go under and come back up. Will was slouched over, his head floating in the water, his arms almost zombielike in front of him, not holding on, his back a little hunched. I grabbed him and pulled his head up, once, twice, three times. Thank God there was still a little light. Otherwise I wouldn't have been able to see him.

Will was unresponsive. He had that same, scared look, like this was it. There was so much going on. The steering cable kept coming loose from his wrist and I wasn't able to tie it into a knot. Three or four times we lost each other; he went under, and I grabbed him and pulled him up.

"Stay with me," I kept telling him. "I can't do this myself."

The fourth time I pulled him up, he just wasn't there. He had no vital signs. His eyes were shut. I was yelling at him, holding him with my right arm around his back, under his armpit. We were chest to chest. My left hand was holding on to the boat.

"Will, Will!" I kept saying. I must have said his name nine or ten times. I was getting emotional, crying. "Will, be there, please be there—I need you! I can't survive without you!"

I shook him and grabbed his T-shirt and yanked it back and forth. "Why?" I screamed a half dozen times, as loud as I could. "Why?"

I held on to him for two or three minutes, bobbing up and down in the water. We were chest to chest, wedged between the swim platform and the motor. My head hit the motor. I didn't know what to do. I just cried.

I tried to pump his chest and give him mouth to mouth, but there was no way with the waves so rough. I'd get close and then we'd hit heads or a wave would come and he'd rip away.

"Why, God, why?" I kept screaming. "Why? Why?"

Will's head was down, eyes shut.

I kept telling him that I loved him.

I looked at his eyelashes. He had big beads of water dripping off of them. He had a cold, still look on his face. His lips were purple.

It was probably six thirty. By this point, I had had two guys die in my arms, literally die in my arms, and a third one got loose and died seconds later, all within the past twelve hours. The sun was setting. It was definitely cold. My teeth were chattering. I was freezing. Hope was running out. I knew I wasn't going to give up, but there was nothing I could do. Four was down to one. It was just myself. All I could do was wait.

I was holding Will by the hand now. I climbed up on the boat somehow and I kept hold of him. I held his wrist. I wish I could have tied him to the boat. At least we would have had his body. I remember his skin being very cold. He was a lot colder than the water, it felt like. A couple more waves came, and I lost my grip. He was gone.

Unlike Marquis, Will didn't sink right away. I could barely look at him. It was eating me alive, tearing me up. I'd look at him for a second and have to look away. I cried and kept screaming, "Why?!"

Please, God, let this be a bad dream, I thought to myself. Let me wake up already. Let Will be alive.

He stayed above water for a while, his head down, slightly slouched, just floating. A wave would come and he would drift above it. It was like he was saying, "I'm not quite ready to go yet."

There were a lot of bubbles coming from beneath his body. For a split second I thought he was still alive. I thought, Oh, my God, I need to go get him. I screamed, "Will, please, Will!" He was twenty feet from the boat, floating away. But of course he wasn't alive. I can't imagine myself feeling worse than that, ever.

I was screaming again, as loud as I could: "Why, please, God, why?!" And I was crying, "I'm so sorry, Will!"

If I had died, I knew how hard it would have been on my family. Will's parents wouldn't even get to bury their child. I would be the last person to see him. I was with Will until the end. I was with all three of those guys for their last words, their last breaths.

I thought about how tough it would be on Will's family. If I got out of this, what would I say to them? I was already speechless. I didn't know his parents well, but I had met them quite a few times. Bob and Betty Bleakley. We used to meet at halftime of USF games. They'd buy us a beer or vice versa, and we'd talk about the game. They were big fans. They never missed a game once Will started playing. It was really hard not to like them. They always wanted to make sure Will was okay.

I pictured all the families. I had only met Marquis's wife, Rebekah, once or twice. I had never met Corey's family. I just kept picturing each family, huddling up together and hugging and crying. I got so upset, it made me sick to my stomach. It was an awful thought. I tried to think of something else, but all I could do was picture them hearing the news for the first time. They would be devastated.

I knew I needed to get through this to explain to them what happened. I needed to live long enough to tell the story, even if I was found alive and died later. If I didn't make it, people would tell their own stories, based on rumors. At least I could tell them the facts.

I had lot of mixed feelings. I was emotionally devastated, just shot. I had a beating heart, but that was about it. That was the only feeling I had other than chattering teeth and the pain in my hip flexor, groin, and butt. Sometimes it took getting banged up by the waves to kind of wake me up for a second.

I kept saying to myself, This is just a bad dream. Come on, Nick, wake up already. Problem was, it wasn't a bad dream. I never even got to go to bed.

My throat felt like it was ripping and tearing. It was completely cracked and dried. I felt worthless and useless. I didn't think the whole thing was my fault, but I was the one who invited Will on this trip. It seemed like every time I thought it couldn't get any worse, it got worse. We saw the helicopters and the planes, but they didn't see us. The storm got worse, the waves got bigger. We saw land, or thought we did, but there was no way we were going to be able to get near that land. Then Will got sick and died.

It was starting to get dark. I thought I deserved a break. Maybe things would get a little easier. It wasn't happening. I was getting sicker and sicker. I hoped I would be found, but I experienced what no person should have to experience. It was terrible. I felt awful.

There's only one thing left, I thought to myself. Three are gone. Now it's my turn. It's just a matter of time.

As horrific as it was, I had no one to worry about but myself now. I didn't have any choice but to go on. People say all the time, "I can't, I can't, I can't," but when you don't have any alternative but to go on, to keep fighting, you'd be surprised what you can do. Strange things started going through my head: "Is there anyway I could eat a bite out of my arm? Is there a way I could drink this water, just a little bit, and not get sick?"

I got back on the boat. I knew if I was going to die, I was going to die sitting there. I felt terrible and I was in pain, but I knew if I wasn't going to make it out alive, it wouldn't be because of the elements or because I drowned. It would be because I starved to death or become so dehydrated it killed me.

I thought I was fighting enough—and aware enough—to survive. I had always wanted more, earned what I got on the field, in the gym, in my life's work. But what if I didn't make it? I thought again about my mother. I knew how hard it would be on Will's family that he was gone. And on Marquis's and Corey's families. Now it might be a matter of time before my own family felt that same awful loss.

Will kind of floated until I couldn't see him anymore. The boat shifted and he was kind of behind me. I couldn't see him for a couple of minutes, then I saw him again. He was still in the same position, floating, head down. After a while, I could see him less and less. We just slowly drifted away from each other. He would go up a wave, then down. And then I couldn't see him. The skies were overcast, no more sun. It was getting dark.

"I love you, Will," I said one final time. I stared and shook my head. I was hugging the motor, holding on to my last hope.

Part III

The next few hours were hazy.

I had been awake for almost forty hours, in the water for more than twenty-four hours, going through the worst elements I could think of, fighting for my life, trying to help three others fight for theirs. I was starving and drained. I couldn't keep my eyes open, but I don't think I ever fell completely asleep, at least not for long. My eyes would shut, and I'd doze; and then I would be startled awake by a wave.

It was dark, maybe seven thirty, and very cold. The waves were a lot smaller than they had been. They were swells, but they felt spaced out a little more. It was still a little choppy, but at least it was predictable. I could feel the cold air on my back, and I pulled the drawstring on my winter jacket as tight as I could.

I kept thinking about Will floating away, and Marquis and Corey dying, and I kept asking, Why? I didn't know why. I didn't have time to grieve, though. I thought I was next. I thought my body was shutting down. Physically, I wondered if I had anything left.

The pain I felt in my stomach was dry, gnawing, and constant, like a stomachache times twenty. I was starving and thirsty. I thought about what I would give for certain meals. If I could have one meal, what would I have? It was my mom's eggs Benedict. She'd make me four or five eggs on an English muffin, covered in Hollandaise sauce with a little lemon in it. It was my favorite breakfast. Perfect.

I locked my arms around the motor. If a wave came from the front and ripped me off the boat, that was okay, because I just swept into the water in a limp gymnastic tumble. As usual, if it came from behind it would lift me off my ass and throw me forward and hammer my genitals against the outboard. The pain was excruciating. It felt like someone with a steel-toed boot was kicking a field goal right into my business. And then I would fly forward, almost body-surfing on the motor, the propeller on my stomach. My neck was rubbed raw from my life jacket. My hands and feet had cuts and gashes. Somehow I never lost my sandals, so at least the bottoms of my feet were protected. But that seemed like a flimsy safeguard. Night had closed in, and now I was alone. My chances of getting rescued, already small, were getting a lot smaller.

I WAS DELIRIOUS. The next two or three hours felt like an eternity. Even with the swells and the bucking of the boat, it was hard to keep my eyes open for more than five seconds at a time. I tried to sleep, but I was afraid to sleep. I might lose my grip and fall off the hull or the boat could go under and drag me down with it. Or I might not see a plane or a boat or a helicopter if they came by and I would miss my chance to get rescued.

I had a good position on the boat. It was horrible that I was alone, and I felt awful for thinking this way, but there was no one else to worry about now, no one to keep an eye on or grab hold of.

It was probably the most beautiful night I had ever seen. The stars were so bright and clear. There was only a sliver of moon, but it seemed super-bright. There were hundreds and hundreds of stars. Thousands. I looked at the moon and stars and thought my mom and dad and sister and Paula had probably looked up at that same moon and stars tonight. I didn't have anything else to do but look and hope and pray.

I'D WAKE UP banging into the motor and I could see blood pouring off my hamstrings and my butt. It would get rinsed away by the water. I hadn't checked the watch—Corey's watch—in forever. When we saw that light from a helicopter or a boat on the first night, when the four of us were still together, still alive, Corey pressed a button to light the dial on his watch. It was green, almost mint in color. The light didn't work at all anymore, but the sky was so bright, I could see what time it was.

Once, I woke up and checked the watch and I thought, Okay, it's got to be two or three in the morning. But it was only nine thirty. There's no way, I told myself. I'm probably not going to make it through this night. Will had said it early in the morning as if it were a premonition. He had been right. And now I thought I might not make it, either.

I STILL HAD my water-resistant phone in my backpack. I would take it out now and again and somehow it still worked. Quickly and carefully, I dialed 9-1-1. I figured everything else had failed, why not keep trying this? But it didn't work. The same thing happened as before. The screen came on; I pressed send, and it said CONNECTING, dot, dot, dot. Then I tried Paula and my mother again. It kept saying NO SERVICE.

I knew I might not make it, but I wasn't going to quit. No one else had quit. I wasn't going to, either.

THE FIRST NIGHT and the next day, Will kept saying, "I can't believe this shit is happening to me."

I had done dumb things, double backflips on snow skis, jumping off the back of a Jet Ski, backflips off big waves. But to be in this position because of a stupid anchor and rope—especially when we weren't doing anything wrong or bad—was crazy. We were just trying to relax and enjoy one another's company before Marquis left for training camp. It just didn't make sense. Nothing made sense on this trip. We weren't drunk or on drugs. We knew the weather was coming and that it was time to head back.

I thought about how I should be home now, lying in my bed, cuddled up with Paula and our dogs. I thought about all the things I had taken for granted in my life—the vacations, the trips to Disney World at Christmas, how my parents had spoiled me and my sister. We had gotten pretty much anything and everything we asked for.

THAT NIGHT, I probably tumbled into the water a dozen times, my feet flying over my head. The sky was bright, and it wasn't as windy as before—there were random gusts, but the consistent breeze was gone. And the water glowed. I had seen it once before, at a wedding in Naples, Florida. Phosphorescence. If I moved my hand or swirled my feet in the water or if the boat smacked against the waves, it looked like little white Christmas tree lights.

I kept checking the watch. I randomly called 9-1-1 and got the same thing. Always connecting, never connected. As the night went on, I was able to hold myself onboard longer. I was in pain, though. My butt felt swollen from sitting so long on the keel, from crushing forward against the motor. It felt like I was sitting on something raised and very hard. I knew something was wrong back there.

I peed once. It only lasted maybe two seconds, but the warmth felt good against my legs, even though the urine burned my cuts.

I was shivering. My throat was dry. My front teeth were really sensitive, like when the dentist touches them the wrong way or you are not quite numb when you get a filling. I didn't know if I was grinding them down, but my jaws were tight. I was giving myself a headache. I kept licking my lips and rinsing my mouth with salt water. I had the worst chapped lips. And my forehead was so cold. I had lost my skullcap when Will and I tried to swim from the boat. Now it felt like I had an ice-cream headache, a brain freeze.

AT SOME POINT during the night, the water felt warmer than the air. I couldn't explain it. It almost felt like a bath. I didn't jump in, at least not on purpose. It took too much work to get back on the boat. My legs, my ass, everything from my belly button to the back of my knees and my calves, was so sensitive and rubbed raw. It felt like I was missing a layer of skin, and then another layer would get ripped off. I could tell I had deep bone bruises. I wanted to stay on the boat as much as possible. I was too weak. I knew a point would come when I wouldn't have the strength to climb back on the hull. And if I couldn't, there was no longer anyone around who could help me. But it felt so good to put my hands in the water.

I KEPT GOING in and out. Once, I woke up and looked to my left. I saw the brightest city. I blinked a few times. I thought I was hallucinating. But the sky seemed bright above some buildings, maybe on a beach. The glow seemed a couple miles long. It went through my mind a couple times that maybe I was near Cuba or the Bahamas or Puerto Rico. I had no idea. There was a reflection of lights bouncing off the water. They were shaped like stars or crosses, like when you squint your eyes. There was so much water in my face it was hard to tell.

The Coast Guard would later say that maybe I saw a cruise ship, or a cargo ship, or maybe I just had a lot of salt water in my eyes. Anyway, I thought it was land. I questioned myself for what seemed like an hour or two, even though it couldn't have been nearly that long. Is this my shot to make a run for it? How far is it? Can I make it? Should I wait? Am I getting closer to the land? Should I try because I might be getting farther away?

I knew it was a matter of time until I reached a point where I wouldn't survive. The odds were against me. I tried my phone again. Nothing. And then for the first time in a long time, I saw a helicopter. My first instinct—I don't know what made me think of this—was to grab my cell phone and pull up the camera. The helicopter never got that close, but I could hear it. I could see a spotlight. It circled. I saw it for ten minutes and I would flash my camera phone. I'd flash it, then press CANCEL, five seconds between each one, flash and CANCEL, flash and CANCEL, deleting the picture and resetting the camera. With the phosphorescence, the water all around me was lit up. I knew the chances they could see me were slim to none, but no way in hell was I giving up.

It might have been about midnight now. I kept going back and forth about the bright city I had seen. Do I go for land? This could be my last chance. The Coast Guard was looking for a white dot in whitecapped water. Do I sit and wait, which has failed so many times so far?

I decided I wasn't strong enough to swim for it. My best chance was to wait on the boat. It had withstood the pounding of the waves so far, so I figured there was a good chance it was going to stay up, even if it seemed to be getting a little lower in the water. The waves were smaller. I worried, hoping that the fish tank or something didn't open underneath, take on water, and drag the boat down. But I thought it would stay up and that I should stay with it.

After the helicopter circled and got farther away, I put my phone back in my backpack, trying to shield it from the waves. I knew the Coast Guard was still looking for us, even though it was nighttime. If I could just make it to morning, the chances of them finding me were better. I was both encouraged and discouraged. Before, all four of us prayed and said, "Please God, we need a break," but we never got a break. Hours earlier, I thought the only good thing was that Will and I were still alive. Now the only good thing was that I was alive and the boat was still afloat.

I TRIED TO use as little energy as possible, keeping my arms and legs tight to my body and my chin down into my sweatshirt, almost on my sternum. I kept breathing down inside my jacket and sweatshirt and T-shirt, trying to keep my chest warm.

A second helicopter came about an hour after the first. It was the same thing. I reached for my backpack and took my phone out. I kept flashing and flashing. This time, a wave threw me into the water. I held on to the phone, but now it was destroyed. The keypad lit up but the screen was gone. I threw the phone back into the bag.

This was just my luck.

Why me? I thought to myself. These other guys didn't make it out. Am I here just to drag out the inevitable?

I was scared out of my mind. Terrified. It was the same feeling, repeating itself from before, each time with one less person. That same terror and fear when there were four of us. The same fear and terror when it was me and Corey and Will for a short time. I was frightened and discouraged when it was me and Will. Mother Nature took my friends, including my best friend. Now I knew there wasn't much time left unless the Coast Guard found me.

Nick Schuyler sitting on the hull of the overturned boat after forty-three hours in the water. *Photograph by FN Adam C. Campbell, courtesy of the United States Coast Guard*

Nick Schuyler with his sister, Kristen, and mother, Marcia, at a Cleveland Cavaliers game.
Courtesy of the author

Nick Schuyler with his father, Stu, at Nick's graduation from college.
Courtesy of the author

Marcia Schuyler, Nick holding dog Torri, and Kristen Schuyler with dog Chloe.
Courtesy of the author

Will Bleakley, Paula
Oliveira, and Nick Schuyler
at a USF football game.
Courtesy of the author

Will Bleakley after receiving a pass at
the University of South Florida.
Courtesy of the University of South Florida

Will Bleakley, Nick Schuyler, and Scott
Miller tailgating at a football game.
Courtesy of the author

Corey Smith playing
for the Detroit Lions.
AP Images

Marquis Cooper
signing an autograph
while playing for
the Tampa Bay
Buccaneers.
AP Images

OVERDUE 21 ft EVERGLADES

Combined Searches

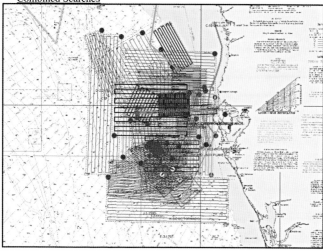

A grid of the Coast Guard searches by boat, plane, and helicopter for the four missing boaters.
Courtesy of the United States Coast Guard

The Coast Guard cutter *Tornado,* which rescued Nick.
Courtesy of the United States Coast Guard

Captain Timothy Close of the Coast Guard, who was in charge of the search, speaks to reporters.
AP Images

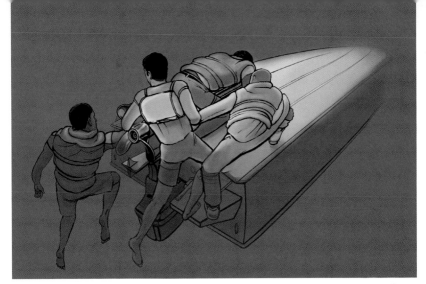

The four men positioned themselves in this way from roughly 6 P.M. Saturday to 4 A.M. Sunday. From left to right: Corey in the water. Will standing on the swim platform wearing the seat cushion. Nick with his left leg on the swim platform, and right leg on the boat with Marquis clinging to it. Marquis on top, lying on the cooler while holding Nick's right leg. *Illustration by John Aymong*

A rescue boat from the Coast Guard cutter *Tornado* speeds out to Nick Schuyler. *Photograph by FN Adam C. Campbell, Courtesy of the United States Coast Guard*

The rescue boat tries to pluck Nick off the overturned hull, but has to back off.
Photograph by FN Adam C. Campbell, Courtesy of the United States Coast Guard

The rescue boat makes another approach as Nick prepares to jump into the water. *Photograph by FN Adam C. Campbell, Courtesy of the United States Coast Guard*

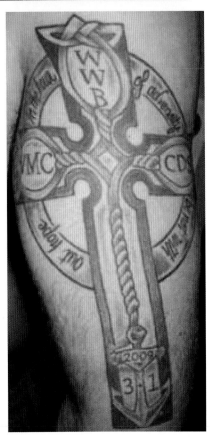

Nick Schuyler gives the thumbs-up upon being hoisted from the *Tornado* to a Coast Guard helicopter.
Photograph by FN Adam C. Campbell, Courtesy of the United States Coast Guard

Nick Schuyler is lifted into a Coast Guard rescue helicopter to be taken to Tampa General Hospital.
Photograph by FN Adam C. Campbell, Courtesy of the United States Coast Guard

The tattoo of a Celtic cross bearing the initials of his deceased friends that Nick got in their honor.
Courtesy of the author

Late Sunday afternoon, Marcia and Kristen Schuyler arrived at the home of Nick, and Paula Oliveira, in Tampa. Paula's mother had also arrived from Fort Lauderdale. The Coast Guard had released the names of the missing boaters. The rest of the afternoon and evening became a blur of phone calls, worrying, and flipping from one news report to the next.

Paula's mother made tea. Paula ate two crackers but could get nothing else down. She felt sick to her stomach. She did not want to upset Nick's mother, so when she felt herself begin to cry, she pretended to receive or make a phone call and walked into her bedroom. Once she took the dogs outside and was struck by how chilly it was. How could they survive this cold on the water? she wondered.

Several times, Paula talked to Rebekah Cooper, Marquis's wife. Rebekah seemed so strong. "They're big guys," she told Paula. "They're so strong. They're in such great shape."

Paula tried to convince herself that they had just run

out of gas. She joked with Kristen, "Nick's going to make it out like they were on *Survivor* and had a little adventure. Here we are, worried sick and hysterical, and he'll come home and make a joke."

Kristen sent out a mass text message to her friends, letting them know that her brother was one of the missing boaters, asking them to say a prayer. She went outside several times to get some fresh air. It had never felt so cold in Florida.

Neither Kristen nor Marcia could sleep. Marcia dozed off a few times in the living room, but then she would awaken and kick the covers off of herself. "I can't be covered and warm and sleeping," she told her daughter, "because my son is out there somewhere, probably freezing." Friends came by with food, but Marcia thought, I can't eat and drink, because he's out there with no food or drink.

She sat in the living room and clenched her fists and repeatedly said, "Come on, Nick, you can do it!" Sometimes she felt guilty because she wasn't saying the names of the other three guys.

At 9:59, Marcia sent Nick a text message: "I luv u so much no u will b safe please stay strong u make me so proud of u!" This was Sunday, March 1. The message would not be delivered until March 5. Marcia kept the message in her phone for the next eight months.

She and Kristen kept calling the Coast Guard, seeking updates. "I'm sorry I'm such a pain, but that's my son out there," Marcia said at one point. The person who answered the phone was gracious each time. At one point, though, Marcia grew impatient when she was told that a cutter had to be pulled back because of twelve- to fourteen-foot seas.

"That boat can't get out there but my son is still out there in those waves?" she said. "You've got to keep a boat out there."

As scared as Kristen was, it never crossed her mind that Nick wouldn't make it home safe. It didn't seem like an option. She never imagined that the boat had turned over. She pictured four guys standing in the boat, getting wet, frustrated that something had gone wrong, but out of harm's way.

She told her mother, "They're probably in the boat, their clothes hanging over the side, drying out, and they're calling each other dumb asses for letting this happen."

Nick had always been a top athlete, Kristen told herself. As a kid, he practically killed himself to be an all-star. At the same time, he was a team player. Making the football team as a walk-on at USF seemed like the biggest challenge of his life.

Kristen had come to visit him in October 2005, when Nick was thinking about returning to school and trying out for the team. He had left Kent State, moved to Florida, and was painting and hanging drywall with his father. He had not played football in five years, but he painted lines on the road to mark off his forty-yard dash and jumped fences at night and ran stadium steps. When he set his mind to something, he always did it, Kristen told herself.

When Kristen had been finishing her undergraduate work at Kent State, Nick had been her personal trainer for a while. He was very intense. He made her run sprints, and if she was off her goal by a hundredth of a second, he would take her water bottle and not let her drink until she ran the designated time.

He would never settle for not completing a task, Kristen thought to herself.

Stu Schuyler went home to Tarpon Springs and glued himself to the television. He called the Coast Guard regularly. He also talked to an old high school friend from Ohio who had served with the Navy SEALs in Vietnam. "Don't give up hope," the friend told him. "If Nick was able to stay with the boat, if he had extra clothes that Kristen said he had taken, if he could pull himself out of the water, he could live two or three days."

Later, Stu turned the television on in his bedroom, grabbed a picture of Nick and held it to his chest. He would doze off and wake up, hearing the wind rattling the screened-in patio. He would cry and say, "God, please help us!"

Halfway through the night, I knew I was dying. I got to a point where I wasn't hungry anymore. I would feel like I was starving and then I wouldn't feel hungry at all. I was so numb, my feet were so numb and painful at the same time. The pain had come back in my feet like on the first night. A sharp pain, especially in my big toes, a constant pressure. It felt like a consistent, real bad stubbing of your toe, like you ran into the couch. I felt like my feet had lost circulation, even though the water felt warm. I could barely move my ankles. My shins were shot, like a layer of skin was scraped away and then a layer under that. There was nothing there. I tried to wiggle my legs and my feet, but they weren't moving. I had tried to hold on for so many hours with my feet and now they were done.

I was aware, but I felt weak. My skin felt wet and soft like I could cut a slice or just pinch it off. I looked at my legs. They were thin. I had lost definition, a lot of muscle. I felt my stomach. I could feel all my ribs. It felt like one of those old-time washboards. I felt my abs, little mounds, absolutely no fat, just skin and muscle on my stomach. It felt like my body fat had dropped from 9 or 10 percent to next to nothing. My job—my life—was to be fit, but I felt like my body was eating away at itself. It was looking for some way to burn fat, but there was no more fat. Now it was eating muscle. I was experiencing things I had never felt before. I thought, This is what dying feels like.

I had used the expressions so many times in my life—"I'm dead tired" or "I'm dead" or "you're killing me"—from a strenuous workout, but that was a cakewalk compared to this. I was dying. I felt almost like a corpse. My heart was still pumping, but I'm not sure how. I rubbed and hit my chest and shoulders and biceps to try to create some warmth, but I didn't want to use what little energy I had left.

My stomach felt like it was being flipped every single way. I felt nauseous. From time to time I got real dizzy. I kept trying to concentrate on what I was thinking about and saying to myself, Oh my God, I'm dying—please, God, help me, I don't have much time left.

I was freezing and I kept putting my hands in the water to warm them. I prayed. "Please, God, find me. If I don't make it out, protect my mom and my sister and my dad and Paula and my dogs."

Thank God I had Will bring my winter jacket. Otherwise, I wouldn't be alive right now. It was water-resistant and somewhat insulated. I kept going back and forth about the land. Or what I thought was land. It seemed like I was getting a lot closer and then it seemed like I drifted past it. I was to the left of it then to the right of it. It was in front of me, then behind me. I knew I was sticking with the boat.

I NOTICED SOMETHING in the water at the stern, a foul smell that lasted for about an hour. I didn't know whether it was some kind of fish. It almost smelled like the bait we had used. It almost looked like some kind of animal's waste, like some kind of animal went to the bathroom, like a squid. I couldn't see any animal, but the sky was bright and it looked like there was a cloud against my feet. It almost looked like chum, broken-down fish. It looked half-eaten, half-digested. It smelled. It was thick, a milky, yolky texture. I never saw anything, not fins or tentacles, but I thought to myself, The squid's back; no way in hell I'm going in the water. It was right there, whatever it was. I tried to lift my feet out of the water, it was so gross.

By midnight Sunday, I had been alone for almost six hours. I was awake and not awake, barely able to keep my head up. I was slouched, hunchbacked. I tried to crack my back, but it didn't give me any relief. I was completely out of whack. My butt was causing me a lot of pain, forcing me to sit in such an uncomfortable position that I could never relax. I kept hugging the motor, my feet under a trim tab or the swim platform, constantly fighting to stay on the boat.

Every time I ended up in the water, it was an immediate shock. I jumped back onto the hull as quick as I could. It didn't feel that bad, but there was no hanging in the water, as warm as it was. I had seen that cloud in the water and smelled that awful smell. So I sat on the hull and tried to stay as dry as possible.

The waves were five to seven feet, choppy. All you could hear were waves breaking and hitting the boat or flying against my back or hitting me in the face. I was so tired. I thought, Are these my last few hours?

I kept thinking about Will, how close I was to him. I thought about Marquis and Corey, too, but losing your best friend in your arms is a lot different. Part of the reason I was still alive was definitely because of Will. He had sacrificed himself and devoted himself to being a leader. We probably wouldn't have had life jackets without him. I can't imagine that the Gatorade and the pretzels worked against me. Those extra few calories coated my system and gave me just enough energy. Working with him that second day, just the two of us, I wouldn't have wanted anyone better. The four of us had worked as best as we could, but Will had definitely helped to save my life to that point.

He always had ideas and was planning things, saying, "Let's do this and that." He was a good student, a smart football player. Always got his work done on time. Always attended class. Always came on time for meetings. He just said, "Yes, sir," to coaches, or if he didn't know something, he'd ask. He was a joy to coach. He just went out every day and tried to get better.

He always had a list of things to do. I was the same way. If we went camping, I wrote down every item we needed to bring. Everything. Food we had in the house, food we needed to buy. A very intricate list: two comforters, three pillows, dog leashes. We would never forget anything, even utensils. We always brought two spatulas, just in case. Will never came shorthanded. We'd always have enough food for two extra days. When we tailgated, we always had food for stragglers: "Here, have a beer and a brat." He was always up for a good time.

Without Will, this night in the water seemed much longer than the first one. There was no one to talk to. Time expanded. When I thought the sun should be coming up, it was only three o'clock. I would think, okay, it's been an hour since I looked at the watch and it would be only twenty or twenty-five minutes.

I FELT AN urge to go under the boat to see if I could find something to eat or drink. My hunger had returned. My body was eating away at anything I had left. All the fat was burned and now it was eating at the muscle. I was dying. I knew I had to make one last-ditch effort to get some water or something to eat. I knew that when you didn't get the proper nutrients your organs got damaged, like when you were anorexic or bulimic.

I had moved past the city I saw earlier—the glow from Tampa, maybe, or a cruise ship or whatever it was—and once again it was dark. I prayed, "Please, God, find me. I won't quit on you." And I said, "I love you, Mom. I won't quit on you."

I kept remembering what Corey had said the first night: "No way in hell I'm going out like this."

The dull repetition continued all night. I'd doze, and then a wave would shoot needles up my back and startle me awake. My cheeks were frozen. My forehead was cold. My lips felt like I had licked an ice-cube tray and ripped away the skin. I kept trying to get low in my jacket, chin to chest, the way a bird burrows into its wing. I kept adjusting my right leg, lifting it off the hull, or trying to straighten it. I had used that leg to cradle Marquis, and now it felt useless. I shrugged my shoulders and pumped my chest. I tried to turn it into a miniworkout. I would shrug my shoulders up to my ears, working my traps. I'd do that 100 times—it just burned. I'd pump my chest 50 times. Same thing with my calves. I'd flex my calves and count to 100 or 150. I didn't count out loud, but sometimes I moved my lips just to pass the time. I did that a few times through the night, trying to create blood flow and warmth. I knew it wouldn't be bad for me. At the same time, I thought, Don't use too much energy. I didn't have anything to refuel with.

Sunrise. It looked like a bright circle coming right out of the water. It was Monday, March 2. The sky was a little overcast. It was definitely warmer at dawn than at midnight. The waves were a little less choppy and more like swells again. There was a random gust of wind every minute or so, but it was better now than before.

I was still going in and out. I was definitely delirious. My head was down, resting on my hands on the motor. I was daydreaming, right at sunrise. Hallucinating. I heard someone yelling, then I realized it was me. I caught myself.

I was on a boat and the other guys were also there, behind me. I was in my spot, at the stern, straddling the motor, facing out to sea. Marquis and Corey and Will were about ten feet behind me, toward the front of the boat. They were standing there. My side of the boat was upside down, but theirs was right side up. They stood under the canopy, driving the boat. I screamed at them. I wanted a gallon of water. "Water, water!" I yelled, long, loud, and mean. I was angry, pissed. I would yell loud and then it would get louder for a few seconds. "Water, water, water!"

They didn't say anything. They were facing me, just their faces, not their whole bodies. I screamed, "Water, damn it!" I felt they were playing a game, ignoring me, giving me a hard time, like, "Too bad, dude, you can't have it."

I reached back with my right hand, holding on to the motor with my left hand, my head down, my eyes closed. I reached like they might hand me something. I could see a clear plastic jug they were going to give me. They were messing with me. They wouldn't hand it over.

Then all of a sudden I popped my head up. I was very alert, very aware. I had never felt that way before. I thought, Oh my God. Holy shit, I'm losing it. I was getting cuckoo. This must have been the same exact thing that happened to Marquis first, then Corey, and finally to Will. And now it was happening to me.

I was frightened to a new level, if that was possible. I tried to stay awake, doing my little exercises. I forgot about being cold and hungry. I was trying to wake up. I thought hypothermia or dementia, or whatever it was, was setting in. I knew this was the first stage of drifting away. My mind was shutting down.

I WAS SEEING things, making random yells. This is what Marquis and Corey and Will had done. It wasn't that they went AWOL or gave up. They had no idea. Their minds were shot. They lost it because of dehydration and hypothermia. And it could happen to me. It was happening to me.

Please, God, come on, come on, I thought to myself. I knew I had to get under the boat. I had to find something to eat or drink, a turkey sandwich, or peanut-butter-and-jelly or a jug of water. I thought there was a case of beer or two still stored under there. I knew I had to go under or nothing would change. I would just wait there until I died. But I knew I wouldn't go without one last fight. I knew the elements wouldn't kill me, but dehydration or starvation could.

I tried to stand a little on the hull and straighten my legs. My hamstrings were so tight, my posture was so bad. My back was so tight, it felt like it was in a brace. I took a look at my legs. They were very white, kind of chalky and pasty from being in the water so long. Particularly my feet. I would shift my legs to get some circulation going. I tried to stand, but all I could really do was put my stomach against the motor and try to lean forward a little to stretch my legs and back.

The sea wasn't so rough, and the water looked a lot clearer. The waves weren't breaking, really. They were round and they would lift the boat up and it would smack back into the water. The water was a lot bluer and clearer. It was darker in some areas, lighter in others. The sun was out. It was a lot warmer. It must have been eight or nine o'clock in the morning. While I stretched, I kept thinking about what I would do to get under the boat.

I still had the steering cable tied to the motor. I could tie off my life jacket and backpack. But where had Marquis put all that stuff onboard? I would only have a few seconds to find anything. Would I be able to see under there?

I must have thought about it for an hour. I had to get things together or this was it. I had to at least try to find something. It would only get worse. No way it would get better. I had nothing to eat, and I wouldn't dare try to drink seawater. In elementary school, we had watched *The Voyage of the Mimi* in class. We'd watch a half-hour segment each day. These people were on a giant sailboat and they were out doing research on whales. Toward the end, they got in a bad storm and the boat was shipwrecked and they were on an island and ran out of supplies. The younger kid, the teenager on the boat, said, "That's okay, I'll drink the salt water," and the captain said, "No, you can't." They built a campfire and they boiled the water, or they put salt water in a bowl and put a trash bag over the bowl, and when the water evaporated, the condensation stayed on the bag and dripped down and they were able to drink it.

I kept looking at my watch. I hadn't eaten anything in the water except a few little pretzels and a half bottle of Gatorade. I had had pasta on Friday night, then cereal and a protein bar on Saturday morning, but I lost all of that. Now it was Monday, two days later. I was empty.

Another helicopter flew by. I waved my life jacket. It was far away and I only saw it for a short time. It moved in the opposite direction that I was facing. That brought me a little hope. At least they were still out looking for us. It was daytime now, I would be easier to see. At least I hoped so.

I was encouraged and discouraged, that same awful feeling from the first time we saw a helicopter, or a light, that first night. Now there was a little less excitement. I knew the chances of them finding me were slim to none. At the same time I thought I would persevere and somehow get out of this. At least the Coast Guard was still looking. As long as they were looking, I wasn't going to quit.

I thought again of my mother, crying next to my coffin. I could picture her hugging my sister, and my dad with both of his arms around their backs. My mom had on a black dress. I saw a room with a coffin and the three of them. My mom was crying "Why, why?"

Again, I wondered who would attend my funeral. I thought about the people I was close to, from my grandmother to my friends. I thought about them hearing the news. I wondered if my ex-girlfriends would show up. I pictured their faces, like in a yearbook. I thought about my aunts and uncles. I thought about my aunt Sue.

She was my mother's oldest sibling. She had ovarian cancer when I was trying out for football at USF. That August, during two-a-days, it was so hard, really hard, for my mother. I had loved visiting my aunt when we were young. We would come to Florida and go to Naples to visit her and Uncle Ben. I saw a lot of my mom in her. She was very funny. We'd play cards a lot. She always asked if I was hungry. She put food or sweets out for me, always made me breakfast. Her house always smelled so clean. It was the smell I thought of when we were going to Florida.

My uncle had a very successful business, concrete, one of many. When Aunt Sue got sick, I missed some practices. The team prayed for her. She died that fall. She was in the hospital and was gone within a month. She was too weak to take chemotherapy. I thought about how bad I hurt when we lost her. And how bad my mom hurt. And how much worse it would be for mom if she lost her son. I said, "Aunt Sue, if you're up there, I could use your help right now."

I said to myself, Dear God, I'll do anything. I thought about Marquis and Corey and Will and I said, "Guys, if you're up there. . . ."

I HELD THE cross I was wearing around my neck. I had the chain since high school. At first it had my basketball number, 31, on it. Then I got a little football with my USF number, 41. After I left the team, I felt it wasn't the right thing to wear anymore. I mentioned to my sister that I wanted something a little different. The previous Christmas, she had given me a simple cross. I put the cross in my mouth. It tasted cold and salty.

* * *

I STILL HAD a nasty taste in my mouth, morning breath times five. I would wash it out with water but I never swallowed. I had phlegm in my throat and my nose was stopped up. I felt like I had a cold or the flu. I knew I was getting worse and worse and I had to get under the boat. I had to overcome my fear of going under the first night. This was my last-ditch effort.

I went back and forth, wondering what it would look like under there. I had never opened my eyes in salt water before. I didn't know if I would be able to see very well. I didn't know if Will had opened his eyes or just reached around blindly. I figured it would sting and burn, but that's not what I was afraid of. I was afraid of getting stuck underneath and not coming up. If I was feeling 100 percent, it would have been a whole different story. Or even 50 percent. Or if it had been in normal conditions, not with waves pushing the boat up and down and me not eating and drinking or sleeping in forever. Now it was different. I was alone. If I got stuck under there, no one could help me.

I ran through it so many times. I was very afraid. Strengthwise, I knew I was extremely limited. Going in the water without a life jacket would be pretty scary. I thought about calling 9-1-1, then remembered that my phone was ruined. I tried it anyway, but there was nothing there. I had Will's phone and his wallet in my bag, too, but his phone had been ruined from the beginning—it never worked. I opened his wallet and looked at his ID. "I'm sorry, Will," I said. "I love you."

I took the steering cable and ran it through my life jacket and backpack and tied them off at the motor. I tried to tie a double knot, but my hands—beat-up, cold, and cut-up—were so weak and inflexible that it was hard to make a tight knot. I lifted my legs and there was blood going down my calves. My legs from the knees down were swollen and cut. My butt felt like it was elevated, like I was sitting on a two-inch piece of jagged metal and it was digging into me. I was so uncomfortable. I'd try to shift my body weight but the crack of my butt was very tender after sitting on a fiberglass keel for two days. It had become almost unbearable.

Before I jumped into the water, I tried one more time to picture the canopy and the cooler under the captain's bench. It was a white cooler with a front clasp, a big handle on each side, bungeed down. Our feet sat on the cooler when we were on the captain's bench. I knew I had to be careful. There was nothing to hold on to. I knew that once I went under, I might not be coming back.

I took my sandals off and put them in the backpack. I wedged the life jacket and the backpack between the motor and the swim platform, lifted my leg over the motor, and slipped into the water. I tried to go slow, the way you go down a ladder into a pool, but the boat was rocking back and forth and I was so weak that I just dropped in. The water was cold again, not warm like the night before. My feet felt frigid. I got nailed by a couple of waves. I tried to keep my head up, then realized it didn't matter—I was going under the boat anyway.

The water was cold and the salt stung my cuts. My whole body was stiff. I floated for a few minutes next to the boat. My lower body felt like one big cut, a raw scab, road rash.

I got as used to the water as I could and made my way to the side of the boat, trying to find something to hold on to, losing my grip. The part of my body beneath the surface moved like a duck, paddling and trying to swim and kick, but nothing was working. It was like I was at an amusement park and I was swimming the wrong way against the lazy river. I'd ride up and down on the swells, which were about five to eight feet. I was cold, more exhausted than ever. The waves slammed me against the boat. I felt I was wasting my energy. My hip flexor wasn't working. I was very alert, though. I knew this was my last try.

I swam as fast as I could to position myself. I knew it was going to be next to impossible to get underwater. I felt too buoyant, almost inflated, in my sweatshirt and my orange winter jacket, but I was too cold to take them off. I prepared to dive, but as soon as I opened my mouth to take a deep breath, I got nailed by a wave. I took in a bunch of water and began coughing and gagging.

The second attempt, I timed it better and waited until the wave went by. I grabbed the railing and shoved myself beneath the boat. I opened my eyes and the water was clear and everything looked like I thought it would look. A lot of things were missing. I saw the gas cans still bungeed down. The fishing rods on the top of the canopy were gone. Other poles were still latched into grooves on the side of the boat. I could see the cooler and the red bungee cord, sitting between the deck and the captain's chair at the center console. It was a big, white Igloo cooler, the same one where Will had found the Gatorade on Sunday. I knew there had to be sandwiches in there, snacks, more Gatorade, water, something.

I just about got to the cooler, but not quite. I just touched it and my heart felt like it was going to pop out of my chest. Just as my feet went under the boat, I slammed my back against the railing. It didn't hurt but it threw me off. I felt like I was already out of breath, like I had swum back and forth across a pool under water. When I was a kid, my sister and I would see who could swim the farthest under water, or who could hold our breath the longest. I always hated it. I didn't like the way my body felt, my chest. Now I felt like I was about to drown. I was under maybe five seconds. I came back up, gasping for air.

I swam to the stern to regroup so I could give it one more try. It was hard to catch my breath. I didn't do a lot under the boat, but that was the most winded I had been in my life. I had been through two-a-days, wearing pads in hundred-degree weather and it wasn't like this. I was cold, and I couldn't catch my breath.

I waited a few minutes behind the boat, holding on to the

motor. I had one more chance left in me. I knew I couldn't do this half-assed. It wouldn't be easy. When a wave would go by, the boat would rise up and slam down. It had been hard to stay under the boat. The waves wanted to rip you along with them.

I went to the side of the boat again and tried to picture where everything was underneath. I waited for a wave to go by, but I kept getting water in my mouth. I went under, positioned myself at a forty-five-degree angle, put my heels on the inside of the boat and kicked. I reached the upside-down cooler and pulled the lid down maybe an inch. The bungee was tight and I was scared and out of breath and I couldn't get it open more than that. The lid snapped closed.

I swam back to the surface; I was exhausted, absolutely discouraged, helpless—the same feeling I had had for forty hours. I felt like I was about to drown, like my lungs and heart were going to explode. I was breathing so hard and had such bad chest pains that I thought my heart was going to pop through my ribs. I took deep breaths quickly, one after the other, like I had just run sprints.

I went to the stern and saw something about fifty feet away, off the back of the motor. It was my life jacket. It had come untied and was floating way.

There was only one thing to do. I waited for a few seconds, trying to catch my breath, then I went hard after it. I couldn't survive without it. I swam, but I was exhausted and kept going under, coming up, and going back under. It was the worst leg burn I had ever experienced. I had done every imaginable aerobic workout—sprints, running stadium steps—but this was far worse.

I'd be trying to tread water and then I'd be a foot under. "This is it," I thought to myself. "I'm about to drown." Somehow, I kept treading water, slowly making headway. The waves weren't like the day before when they were crashing randomly. I kept getting to the surface and going back under, thinking, I can't get too low or I'll never come up. I tried to relax by doing the breaststroke or swimming freestyle, whatever hurt least at the moment. I gave about ten more big kicks and paddles with my arms and got the life jacket. I threw it underneath my stomach so it could hold me up, and swam back toward the boat. It took me twice as long to get back.

The backpack was still wedged against the motor, loosely. I put the life jacket on and just floated there, wanting to get out of the water but completely out of breath. My heart pounded so hard. I didn't think I could pull myself onto the hull. I just concentrated on my breathing for five minutes. It didn't get any better. I had to get out of the water, though, so somehow I swung my right leg over the motor and slammed my butt on the keel. I was in so much pain.

I thought I was down to my last few hours. It had already gone through my head that I was dying, but now I felt like I was going to die right there. My breathing didn't change for forty-five minutes. Deep, deep, quick breaths. My heart rate felt like it was 180 beats a minute. It was pounding and wouldn't stop. I didn't know if I was going to have a heart attack or maybe even an asthma attack. I started to panic.

I took the steering cable and tied it as tight as I could to the motor and to my life jacket. I didn't know if they had found the other guys yet, or if they ever would. But this way, if I had my life jacket on and I was tied to the boat, somebody would eventually find it. And unless something ate me, they would find me, too.

I kept wondering if there was a way I could leave some kind of message, something like "Love you, Mom," or "Love you, guys" or "Be happy" or "Be strong." I thought about my parents, my sister, and Paula. If only I had a pen in my bag. I wanted to let someone know that the boat flipped because of the anchor. I wanted there to be a way to explain how hard we had fought and how we just didn't give up. It wasn't like there was an explosion on the boat and we flipped and all died then and there. I wanted them to know how long we fought, how we worked together, how we depended on one another to survive, how three helped when one got bad, then two helped when two got bad. Just the whole story. I knew that wasn't possible on a sheet of paper. If I had a pen, I could have written on my arm. I wondered if there was a way I could cut myself on the prop and engrave a message on my arm or my body: "I love you guys." Then I thought I might bleed to death right there.

My nose was running—the snot tasted salty—and I kept wiping it with what was left of my cotton gloves. I forgot all about the cold, almost like I wasn't cold anymore. All my attention went to my breathing. Or I'd lean one way and then the other, trying to shake water out of my ears. My teeth were chattering, my lips were raw and blistered inside and out. I gargled with salt water, just to get some moisture in my mouth.

Finally, my heart rate slowed down. All of a sudden, it went from this race car to a slow turtle. I was straddling the motor, slouched over. My head was down on my hands. I could barely keep it up. I'd get thrown forward a bit, but for the most part I rode the waves up and down. Once my heartbeat relaxed, I started breathing so slow, like when I was sleeping. It scared me. I would gasp for air, like I was biting it, trying to get more oxygen.

I said my final words: "Please, God, protect my family. Give my dad the strength to figure out whatever makes him happy. Tell him I love him, and I'm proud of him regardless of some of the mistakes he had made in past. I love him and my sister loves him, too.

"Please help my sister find a good man, someone to protect her and love her and take care of her and make her feel like the great girl and fun, outgoing person she is.

"Dear God, protect Paula, give her the strength to get through this. Let her know I've always loved her and always will. Let her know I appreciate her even though I didn't always show it. Help her find a man down the line who will make her happy and love her like I did."

I said all this out loud.

I could picture my mom.

"Dear God, give her the strength to get through this and give her someone who can make her happy. I just want her to be happy. I love her, and she was the best mom I could ever ask for. I'm so proud of her."

My heart rate was so slow. I felt like my body was done, I couldn't go any longer.

Then I saw a boat.

I could see an orange racing stripe on the boat, so I knew it was the Coast Guard emblem. But was I seeing an actual boat? Was it a mirage? Was I so desperate to be rescued that I imagined the ship? I had already hallucinated, so maybe I was doing it again. But there it was, a boat in the distance. I tried to stand as much as I could on the hull. I took my life jacket off and swung it when I got to the top of a wave. The boat was a mile away, at least. I'd see it for a second and I'd go down the backside of a wave and lose it. Am I really seeing this? I kept asking myself.

This went on for twenty minutes or so. I'd see the boat and swing my life jacket and lose it behind a wave. I was choked up, upset. Please, God, please, I kept saying.

I tried to scream, "Help!" once, but my throat was shot, and the scream was smothered in my mouth. It was useless anyway. The boat was real, but it was too far away. It kept moving farther away and all of a sudden it was gone.

That's it, I thought.

I hadn't seen any choppers since early morning. I had done

what I could to get under the boat. I had said my prayers to my family. This was it. I was in my last few hours.

I began to think again about the things I would have changed in my life. I should have stuck with football. I should have been better to my mom. I should have spent more time with my dad. I should have kissed Paula one more time before I left.

I wished I hadn't invited Will on this trip.

It was hard to focus, I'd get so sidetracked. I would be coherent for a while, then out of it for a second. I'd come back and look up. I felt like I was drugged up. Had I gone to the bathroom in my swimsuit? I stood up and shook my shorts and reached inside to get it out. There was nothing there. I couldn't tell if I went.

I felt like I had more swelling around my butt. I felt I was sitting on an inch of iron or a brick. It was so raw and tender. My whole ass felt like a scab that had been ripped open. Blood was in the water, dripping off my legs. I felt light-headed, more than usual. I thought I was going to bleed to death. Okay, I thought, my ass is literally falling off. My insides are eating away at me. This is just another way that you die. I was the living dead. I couldn't sit flat anymore. I'd put the majority of my weight on one cheek, then the other. I wanted to cry, but I didn't have the energy even to do that.

I had always told people that crying didn't solve any problems, didn't make you feel better. Now I wanted to cry, but I didn't have the strength.

I was coughing a lot. It hurt my ribs. It felt like I had to vomit, but there was nothing to throw up. It would have been straight bile or blood. I worried that I was bleeding internally from banging against the boat. As blood kept dripping in the water, I knew I needed to stay on the hull in case any sharks came back.

* * *

I WENT IN and out of consciousness. I had forgotten about the cold. My whole attention was on the pain in my butt. I'd try to lean forward on my hands to get a little relief. Then I would fall asleep for a minute, a random wave would come, and I'd hit the motor with my crotch, which would startle me awake. The boat seemed to be getting lower, losing some of its buoyancy. As I sat on the hull, water washed over my butt.

I felt woozy. I put my head down on my hands, which were holding on to the motor, and I put my cross in my mouth. I looked at my legs; it seemed like my calves were an inch and a half bigger. They were swollen, bruised, and pale. The little cuts on my legs had scabbed and were soggy and pruned. My ankles were fatter and had no shape. I had lumps on my shins.

I had been in the water about forty-two hours. I was both awake and not awake. The cold was gone. I knew I was starting to lose it, but I never lost my pain. It was direct and ceaseless. It shot down my back, through my whole body. I couldn't straighten my back. My posture was gone.

I straightened out my right leg, but something wasn't right. It was tight and sore, and I didn't have a lot of movement with it. This was my last couple of hours, I figured. I made sure the steering cable was tied tightly to my life jacket. If I died, I'd be within a couple feet of the boat when they finally found me.

I went through the whole story one more time: Marquis's face right before I let him go. The dark of the night and the grueling sounds, the constant blowing of the wind and the waves crashing against the boat. Marquis's cold, hard face, his eyes closed, head fallen to the side. Corey's last words, "I'm a kill you"—mean, wide-eyed, the words coming from his mouth but not from his mind. I knew it wasn't him, but I wished those weren't his last words.

I remembered the few words Will had said: "I love you." His face was the saddest. He was defenseless—the water dripped off his face and his nose was running. That was even worse than letting go of Marquis.

I said it again now, "I love you, Will," and I pictured him saying it back.

In my head, I saw my family and Paula at my funeral, in front of the coffin, crying, holding one another. Later, I would tell my sister that I thought I saw my friend from Ohio, Nate Milstead, the cop from Akron. He was standing on shore at Shephard's Beach Resort on Clearwater Beach, near the spot where we caught our bait fish early Saturday morning. I guess I thought I was on a boat, ready to dock, or I was swimming in the water. I could see Nate on shore and I kept telling him, "Come pick me up, come get me, I'm so close!"

ABOUT ELEVEN THIRTY I was slouched down, straddling the motor, head in my hands, when I heard something crashing. It was the same crashing noise the boat made when it went up a wave and flopped back down against the water, but it was louder and it didn't sound like it was close.

I moved my head to the left, eyes half open, and I caught something in the corner of my eye. It was a boat, a big gray boat. I put my head back down. I'm seeing things, I thought. I shook my head and closed my eyes and opened them wide. The boat was still there.

I turned my head even more. I could barely keep my eyes open. I just stared for about ten seconds. I tried to yell, but my throat was dry, blistered, and closed up. "Over here, over here!" I whispered.

I took off my life jacket and stood as much as I could. I didn't have the strength to get all the way up, so I really just leaned forward against the motor. I swung my life jacket over my head. If they hadn't seen me, I was going to get in the water and try to swim toward them. I was already more than dying.

The boat kept getting closer. "Thank you, God, thank you, God," I began saying. I probably said it twenty times. "Oh my God, thank you. I can't believe it."

This boat was big and gray and I could see the orange Coast Guard emblem again. I was thinking, How the hell am I going to swim and get on that boat?

The Coast Guard cutter *Tornado* had been on routine patrol in the Florida Straits, off the coast of Cuba, operating on one engine in quiet seas, nothing pressing on a Sunday afternoon. Its primary mission generally involved law enforcement: restricting the flow of illegal aliens and drugs and preventing illegal fishing, while also checking commercial and recreational vessels for safety compliance. At 2:40 in the afternoon on March 1, though, Lieutenant Commander Patrick Peschka received a change of orders. The *Tornado* was to divert 230 miles northward to assist in a search-and-rescue operation off the coast of Tampa–St. Petersburg.

Many in the crew learned of the new mission from the Internet, said Adam Best, a gunner's mate third class who also served as the *Tornado*'s emergency medical technician.

"We had been diverted to St. Pete; that's all we knew," Best said. "Then, on the Internet, we saw that the Coast Guard was looking for four missing football players. That's where we were headed, so we figured that must be what we were going to do."

Three of the *Tornado*'s four engines were operational, and the cutter picked up speed to twenty-three or twenty-four knots, heading east of the Dry Tortugas. Lieutenant Commander Peschka knew there was bad weather up in the Gulf. He checked the forecast and knew it was a matter of time before the *Tornado* started feeling the affects of the storm. After about ninety minutes, the winds had increased from ten to fifteen miles an hour. By late Sunday afternoon, the wind was blowing twenty to twenty-five miles an hour and the seas were starting to build. Swells rose from three feet to eight feet and the *Tornado* was forced to reduce its speed to ten to twelve knots.

Between midnight and two on Monday morning, the weather got worse. The *Tornado* had to back off its speed a little more. Maximum winds built to thirty-five miles an hour, with twelve-foot swells. Even aboard a ship that was 179 feet long, some of the crew began to get seasick, said Michael Briner, the chief boatswain's mate. "You are literally holding on so you don't get thrown around," Briner said.

Some of the crew had a trick for trying to sleep in rough seas. They placed their boots under their mattresses, forming an incline on their twenty-four-inch-wide beds. The incline rolled them toward the walls of the narrow bunks.

David Earles, a boatswain's mate second class, awakened at one point to the sound of a fire hose rolling around the deck. The waves had become so powerful that an ammunition box three feet high and three feet wide was ripped away from the twelve half-inch bolts that anchored it to the bow. Best, the gunner's mate, awakened Monday morning to find the box missing.

"It tore pieces of the boat apart," Briner, the chief boatswain's mate, said of the storm. "Some of the metal parts on board were bent from the waves coming on. There were things we had to weld together afterward."

By three or four on Monday morning, the weather began to improve. By seven o'clock, the *Tornado* had come through the bulk of the storm. Swells still rose to six feet, though, as the cutter began its initial search at 7:45. The search opened in a westerly direction for eight to ten miles, took a northerly turn of a quarter mile to a mile for spacing. and then proceeded in a straight line creep in an easterly direction. It was the equivalent of starting in the end zone of a football field, moving up to the five-yard line, going all the way across to the sideline, edging up to the ten and then going back across the field in the opposite direction.

Usually, there were three lookouts on the bridge, scanning forward, starboard, and port. It would not be easy to spot the hull of a capsized twenty-one-foot boat or a person who sat on the boat or floated in the water. Whitecaps could be indistinguishable from the hull. And plenty of debris floated in open water, everything from milk jugs to old rafts to refrigerators, which could complicate a search. It wasn't the same as standing on flat land and looking into the distance, or peering from a car on the Interstate. On a ship, both the terrain and the vessel were moving. Searching on the water could feel like searching in an off-road vehicle, everything bucking and shaking and the horizon unsteady.

On a flat, calm day, a beach ball might be visible on

the water miles and miles away, Lieutenant Commander Peschka said. But that same beach ball may not be visible one hundred yards off the ship if it kept disappearing in the trough of a wave or the light was too harsh or flat or the ball's color became indistinguishable from the color of the sea.

The Coast Guard was not really afraid that Marquis Cooper's boat would sink entirely if it had overturned, said Captain Timothy Close, commander of the St. Petersburg Coast Guard sector. Everglades model boats were built with a system called the Rapid Molded Core Assembly Process, or RAMCAP. This process bonded the hull, deck, and structural core together under extreme pressure in a way meant to keep the boat afloat even in the harshest seas. On conventional fiberglass boats, foam was injected or sprayed between the deck and hull to create buoyancy. In the RAMCAP system, a premolded, high-density, closed-cell urethane core was chemically bonded to the hull. The chemical bonding formed pockets, or cells, of air that were like closed bubbles. Think of it like Styrofoam, Captain Close said, a closed-cell product that does not absorb water, compared with a sponge or a foamy seat cushion, open-celled items that do absorb water. Even if Cooper's boat was still afloat though, it could be extremely difficult to spot.

While peering through binoculars, Coast Guard crewmen were taught to move their eyes in a repeating S shape, over and down, over and down. Without binoculars, they also moved their eyes back and forth, like the carriage of a typewriter. Lookouts generally started from the horizon and worked their way toward the boat. They were taught to vary their methods, sometimes starting at the bow and working toward the horizon so their eyes wouldn't become tired and strained.

"That old saying about seeing the forest for the trees, well, in a search on the water, the detail you're trying to get down to is seeing an individual branch," said Lieutenant Commander Peschka, who was thirty-seven. "Trying to find Nick was not like looking at a tree but at a branch."

Chief Boatswain's Mate Michael Briner, who was thirty-nine, used the dozen windows on the bridge of the *Tornado* to help frame his searches. He started at the waterline, or just above or below it, divided a window into sections, and began his scan, sweeping his eyes left to right. Even with sophisticated technology, there was no more valuable equipment in the Coast Guard than the human eye.

"What I've always been taught is, electronics fail when you need them," Briner said. "That's why we need the people out there. They make the difference."

He knew from his sixteen years in the Coast Guard that objects were more quickly located with peripheral vision than direct staring. Twice Briner had been involved in rescues. Eleven or twelve years earlier, off of Florida's Atlantic coast, he had spotted two divers who had been in the water, away from their boat, for three days. In 2006 a family on a small boat ran out of gas fifty yards from the shoreline of Lake Superior, only to be blown back out into the lake. After an initial search failed to locate the family, Briner and Coast Guard colleagues initiated a second search and found the boaters after they had been stranded for eight hours.

On this Monday morning, he had stood watch on the *Tornado* from midnight to four, gone to sleep, and awakened at nine thirty. In late morning, he went up to the bridge with a cup of coffee to see the daylight and stretch his legs. Three lookouts were on duty, and Briner joined them in scanning the water. Coast Guardsmen are taught that anytime they are on the bridge, they are to look out the windows, whether they are on duty or not. Even on a cigarette break, they are expected to lend an extra set of eyes.

At 11:43 in the morning, about thirty-eight miles west of Tampa, Briner saw a speck of orange and a white wave that didn't go away. The water was rough and the waves would come and go, but this one did not break and disappear. That's an odd place for a buoy, Briner thought to himself. And then he realized that there were no buoys out here.

"I've got something," Briner said to the others on the bridge.

Briner hurried to the window, locking on the object, which was about five hundred yards off the starboard side. If anyone got in his path, he was prepared to shove them out of the way.

"A basketball in the water, that's about as much as you saw," he said.

He leaned into the window, steadying himself, and kept his eyes locked while feeling around for a pair of binoculars.

"Hey, I've got a person," Briner said.

Everything got quiet and others on the bridge scrambled for binoculars, confirming what he had seen: "We've got someone alive."

Everything was in motion now on the *Tornado* with a sense of excitement and urgency.

"I find it very amazing we found him," Lieutenant Commander Peschka said. "But Nick did the right thing, wearing bright colors, sitting on the back of the boat."

Even so, Briner said, "If he would have been on a different crest of a wave, we would have gone right by him."

A general alarm sounded, along with instructions to prepare the cutter's twenty-three-foot rescue boat for launch. The boat was a hybrid, with a rigid, fiberglass hull and an inflatable collar. David Earles, the *Tornado*'s rescue swimmer, was in the mess hall, having just finished lunch. He hurried to the bridge and was told that a person had been found in the water. He went aft and slipped into a short-sleeved wetsuit and a harness with a rope attached. Within a couple of minutes, two stern doors opened on the *Tornado*, and its rescue boat slid down a ramp into the water.

As a four-man crew sped toward the overturned boat, the man on the hull kept disappearing behind a wave, then reappearing. The coxswain, crew members, and rescue swimmer stood as tall as they could to keep the man in their sights. The man was sitting with his head down, shoulders slouched, holding on to the motor. He wore gloves, an orange life jacket, an orange winter jacket, and a sweatshirt, its hood pulled over his head.

Earles, who was twenty-five, had been in the Coast Guard less than two years and had never been called upon to make a water rescue. He never expected to on this search-and-rescue mission, either. Surely, he thought, the missing boaters would be spotted and hoisted out of the water by a helicopter.

The rescuers pulled alongside the man with the intent of grabbing him off the capsized boat. But the seas were six feet, whitecapped, and rough, and the rescuers backed off.

"Are you all right?" Earles asked.

The man said he was.

"Anybody with you?"

There were three others, the man said. They were gone.

The Coast Guard was searching for four men and a twenty-one-foot boat. This had to be one of those four. Earles looked at the man's feet. He had a wrinkled look, like he had been in the bathtub way too long.

Before jumping in the water, Earles told the man, "Don't move, I'm coming to you."

He was ten yards away from the man.

"Can I swim to you?" the man asked.

"No," Earles said. "I'm coming to you."

The man started to move, so Earles said, "Lower yourself in the water."

He reached the man, handed him a flotation device, and told him to float on his back. A crew member on the rescue boat began to reel them in using the rope attached to Earles's harness.

"Relax," Earles said. "I've got you."

Twelve minutes had elapsed from the time the man was spotted by Briner until he was aboard the rescue boat.

O h my God, thank you," I kept saying when I saw the life raft
coming toward me. I could barely keep my eyes open. But I
started to get more feeling back in my body, like I was coming back
to life. I started feeling cold again, and my butt was hurting. The
guy yelled, "Stay right there, we'll come to you," but I was thinking
hell no, I'm not waiting. I pretended not to hear. I didn't care. I had
been sitting on that boat so long, I was getting in the damn water.
They would have had to hit me with a stun gun to keep me from
going in. I was getting ready to swim to the big boat.

The guy reached me and I said "Thank you." If I said it once,
I said it a hundred times. He handed me a red float like you see on
Baywatch.

His left arm was under my left armpit and around my chest.
He was swimming for both of us. I had nothing. They were reeling
us in like fish. He asked if I had any injuries.

"My ass," I told him.

I kept saying, "Thank you." I could barely talk.

They grabbed my life jacket and pulled me out of the water.
Once they got me higher up, they grabbed my swimsuit. I didn't

think I could be in any more pain than I had already been in. But the guy gave me the world's worst wedgie. I flopped in the boat and screamed. They kept asking, "What's wrong with your butt?"

"I don't know," I kept telling them.

They asked me about the others.

"They're gone," I said. "There are no others."

My eyes were pretty much shut. I had experienced so many different feelings in those forty-three hours in the water. Now I had a different feeling, relief and guilt at the same time. Why am I alive? Why am I going to make it out of this? Why was I found and saved and my best friend and two other friends didn't make it? I kept wishing there was at least another person in the rescue boat with me.

It seemed like we got back to the big boat in two minutes. I was laying on my back. "You're going to be okay," one guy said. "You're strong. It's a miracle."

I was so weak, I could hardly walk. Two guys held up 90 percent of my body weight. My feet were swollen. It felt like I was walking on clogs, an inch of rubber. They told me to hold on to the railing. We walked toward the middle of the boat. "We're going to get you inside," someone said. The boat was rocking so far up and down. Two guys held me. I looked down and there was blood on my feet and ankles.

"I'm so cold," I kept saying.

"We're gonna get you inside into some warm clothes," the guy said.

My legs were useless. I had to take little strides. It felt like the muscles were just hanging off my hamstrings and my butt cheeks.

"I'm so thirsty," I kept saying.

Adam Best, the *Tornado*'s emergency medical technician, and David Earles, the rescue swimmer, helped guide the man to the executive officer's bathroom, where he was dried off, stripped of his wet clothing, placed in a pair of Coast Guard coveralls, covered in wool blankets, and given a pair of sandals. The sandals were generally given to migrants plucked out of the water on rafts or small boats. The biggest pair aboard the *Tornado* was a size twelve. This man wore a fifteen.

His temperature was 89.5 degrees, well below the normal 98.6. His breathing was somewhat labored. He complained of being cold and his lips were turning blue. His skin felt cool and clammy. He seemed to be going into the early stages of shock. He also had pain in his legs. He had minor cuts on his legs; the salt water was making them feel worse than they actually were.

Best asked the man standard questions to gauge his alertness. He seemed mostly coherent. He knew his name, Nick Schuyler. He knew where he was and even what month it was, but he could not remember at the moment who was president of the United States.

"As long as he had been out there, he was in better shape than I thought he would be," Best, who was twenty-one, said. "He would laugh, and then he would remember what happened and get serious again."

Michael Briner, the chief boatswain's mate, asked Nick his name again and confirmed that he had been with NFL players. It was a bad storm. There could have been more than one capsized boat. The Coast Guard wanted to make sure it was on the right case.

The *Tornado* phoned the Coast Guard station in St. Petersburg.

"We got him," an officer said to Captain Timothy Close, commander of the St. Petersburg station.

They switched to secure communications.

"Who is he?" Captain Close asked.

He wanted Schuyler's name double-checked. If he was hallucinating and calling out his buddies' names, there could be a mix-up. The *Tornado* reported that Schuyler had a backpack with his wallet inside, verifying his identification.

Nick wanted water, but Best gave him only sips. He didn't want to cause him to go into shock. Plus, Nick was already dehydrated, and if he drank too much and threw up, he could become even more dehydrated.

"You're killing me," Nick kept saying. "Just give me the water."

"You gotta take it slow," Best kept replying.

Nick kept saying his chode hurt.

"Please specify," Earles, the rescue swimmer, told Nick. "I don't know what that is."

His taint, Nick explained. He meant the perineum, the area between his scrotum and anus, which was in extreme pain from sitting on the keel for two days.

One guy asked me, "The others are gone?"

"They're gone."

"Do you know where they would have been?"

"No, they're gone."

"Where did the boat flip?"

"Seventy miles straight out of Clearwater."

I had floated almost thirty-five miles.

I was leaning against a wall in the bathroom of the ship. I didn't want to sit because of my butt, but it was hard to stand because my feet were so sore and my legs were so weak.

When they took my jacket off and my sweatshirt and T-shirt, I could see every single muscle in my stomach. I was shredded. I had deep grooves between the muscles. It looked like I had worked on my abs five hours a day for five weeks. I had zero body fat. I couldn't grab on to the skin. Shit, not bad, I thought to myself.

They gave me a couple small bottles of water. As soon as it would hit my lips, the guy would grab the bottle. I was pissed.

"What are you doing?"

"You can't drink too much too fast."

"I haven't had any for two days."

"Too much is not good for you."

I wanted to push him away and chug it, but he was holding me, and I didn't have the strength.

I asked for a shower and one guy said, "No. We can't raise your temperature too fast, it could kill you."

A guy said they had to get my swim shorts off, but I couldn't lift my right leg, it was so stiff. I looked down: I was a bloody, scabby mess. My penis looked like I was a newborn. It had wrinkles everywhere, a big red strawberry on the head, all of it from nailing the motor. The inside of my legs were full of bruises, cuts, and scabs, all very raw and soggy-looking. I touched my groin and skin came off. I was embarrassed. I slouched as much as I could and they got me another blanket. They gave me a little water. I wanted more.

When they took my clothes off, I felt even colder than when I was in the water. I was naked and shivering. I started getting feeling back in places I had lost it. Someone asked me again, "The other guys didn't make it?"

"No," I said. "They're gone."

"How did the boat flip?"

"The anchor got stuck."

The water they gave me felt like it was a hundred degrees, like bathwater. I wanted ten gallons of cold water, not teeny sips of bathwater. I was excited to be alive, but I had that same guilty feeling. Why weren't my best friend and Marquis and Corey on this ship with me?

They told me a helicopter was on the way and that I'd be airlifted out in a basket. I was scared. A guy said a couple times in a stern voice, "We need to get his temperature up now. We can't let it drop anymore." They kept giving me new, dry blankets.

A guy asked if I was okay. The conversations were short. I could barely stand. From my navel to my lower back, around my butt, it felt like my skin had been ripped off with a knife.

Two guys held me while I put a blue jumpsuit on. It was three sizes too small, but the biggest they had. I wasn't complaining, except that I was cold and wanted water.

They walked me outside. I could barely stand on my feet. The sandals they gave me were way too small. My thighs rubbed together, and it felt like the skin was rubbing off.

When the door to the outside opened, I felt a shot of cold air. My teeth were chattering. I could hear the helicopter hovering over the boat. It was getting louder and louder, real rough out. I was colder than I had been on the overturned boat. A guy hugged me and held a blanket around me.

"Hold on a little longer."

He was screaming and I could barely hear him.

"Another minute," he said, "we'll get you in the basket."

I looked up while they were lowering it, and I thought no way I could fit in that thing. It was about four feet long with a bar looped over the middle, attached to the cable from the chopper. Water was spraying up into the air, and I was so cold that I could barely stand it. They held up my feet and I flopped into the basket and hit my butt—it hurt so bad. There were a million things I wanted to say or scream, but I held it in.

"You'll be all right!" a guy yelled. "Don't move—just hold on!"

Then I was being hoisted up, and people on the boat were staring at me, waving and giving me the thumbs-up. I gave the thumbs-up with my right hand.

I had been on the ship for an hour. When I got up to the helicopter it was windy and even louder. I was so cold. I thought I was going to die from freezing. The chopper guys grabbed me and pulled me inside, still in the basket, slouched over. I wished I was the only one who went into this situation. It would be a good story to tell later, but one out of four is not a good score for anything.

Kevin Lajeunesse, Coast Guard petty officer second class, had been on a shoreline search with his helicopter crew for twenty or thirty minutes. They received a message that the cutter *Tornado* had found one of the missing boaters. The helicopter headed thirty-five miles west of St. Petersburg. A C-130 cargo plane was in the area, looking for survivors and had spotted a couple of things of interest. The helicopter made a low flyover and saw no signs of movement. It then headed for the *Tornado.*

"They were like, 'This guy needs medical attention,'" Lajeunesse said. '"Can you guys hoist him and bring him to Tampa General?'"

Lajeunesse hoisted the man into the chopper and asked him if he was Will Bleakley. He had known from friends that Will was one of the missing boaters.

The man shook his head no.

"How are you doing?" Lajeunesse asked him. "What happened?"

The man said that hypothermia had set in. Corey

Smith had taken off his life jacket. He was traumatized. His eyes weren't right. He sank like a rock. Will had possibly seen a light on the horizon.

The Coast Guard took the man's vital signs. His temperature was rising, but 93 was still low. His skin was scabbed up and covered with dry salt. He looked beaten up and tired. Lajeunesse gave him water. He gulped it down. He was still covered in a thick wool blanket. Lajeunesse directed excess heat that bled off the engine—bleed air, it was called—at the man's head and feet.

In the chopper they asked me the same questions that they did on the ship: How many others? Where are they? Where could they be? Where did you dock out of? How far did you go out?

They gave me three big bottles of water. I was so weak, I didn't want to lift the bottle. I tipped my head back and let the water fall in my mouth.

"Are you sure your friends didn't make it?" someone asked.

"I'm sure," I said.

They asked me if the other guys were wearing life jackets. I said they did but that they had slipped them off.

We were on our way to Tampa General Hospital. I asked if my family and girlfriend had been notified.

"They'll be there."

I had headphones on and it was loud and staticky from time to time. About twenty or thirty minutes after we left the cutter, we landed at the hospital. I grabbed the basket and tried to push myself to my feet. One of the Coast Guard guys helped to lift me up. I saw a couple of guys running out with a stretcher. I was warmer than on the boat, but I was still very cold. I tried to turn myself to one side to keep the pressure off my butt. It was killing me.

All of a sudden I saw reporters and microphones and cameras. I felt like an actor going into a building and everyone is attacking him. It was confusing. One of the reporters yelled, "Where are the others?" Somebody else asked, "How are you feeling?" The rest was just one voice on top of another. Next thing I knew, I was in the ER. They cut my jumpsuit off, threw IVs in both my arms, checked my pulse, and hooked me up to a heart monitor. I could hear machines beeping. I was out of it. I was so cold and exhausted. All I wanted to do was drink water, warm up, and go to bed.

I asked where my family was. They were in the waiting room. I had to see them right away.

As the sun came up on this Monday morning, Kristen Schuyler grabbed one of her brother's sweatshirts and put it on. At least she would have a part of Nick wrapped around her. Her mother, Marcia, did the same thing. Marcia Schuyler also put on a pair of Nick's socks as she sat in the living room of his house, in his favorite recliner, crying, praying, flipping through the channels, still clenching her fists and saying, "Come on, Nick, you can do it."

Early in the morning, Marcia said to her daughter, "Kris, we're in trouble."

"Mom, don't say that," Kristen replied.

Marcia called the Coast Guard and was told that the waves were receding in the Gulf. Boats would be arriving at the search site. At least that was good news.

Paula Oliveira walked into the living room, saw the worry on the faces of Nick's mother and sister, who had not gone to sleep, and said, "Oh, my God, what's wrong? Did you guys hear something?"

"No," Kristen said, "we haven't heard anything. That's the point."

For a long time, Kristen went outside and sat in the driver's side of Nick's Jeep, staring at a guardian angel that was attached to the visor. She had bought it for her brother, hoping it would protect him on the road.

The house began filling with Nick's friends, people going in and out. Paula took her three dogs for a walk. The pets seemed to be crowding around her in the house, as if they sensed that something was wrong in Nick's absence. Paula took them down the street and prayed as she went along. She came home feeling more encouraged.

"All right, I'm going to go shower," Paula said to the dozen friends who sat around the living room and the kitchen. "When Nick comes home today, I'm going to have to look clean and good."

Everyone laughed, if nervously.

A couple of hours later, Paula took the dogs for another walk. Her mother went with her. Marcia Schuyler cried off and on. She knew that Nick would keep fighting. She remembered how he had played basketball in high school with a broken nose. He had taken off his bloody jersey and put a clean one on and had gone right back in the game until he became dizzy and the coach had to pull him out. He had played that same game with a severely sprained ankle, refusing to get an X-ray. He was not the kind to give up. But he was in the Gulf and he had been gone for two days. Kristen sat with Marcia and held her hand and told her that everything was going to be okay. But Marcia was nearly hysterical.

"They have to find him today," she told Kristen. "If they don't find him today, they won't find him."

"Mom, don't say that," Kristen said. "They'll find him."

Marcia took a shower and went back to the television in Nick's living room, changing channels, terrified.

"You gotta stop watching this," Ben Busbee, one of Nick's friends and a tight end on the USF football team, told her.

Kristen spoke with Nate Milstead, another of Nick's friends, the cop from Akron. "You know your brother," he reassured her. "He's out there, he's fighting."

Kristen's boyfriend was with her, along with one of her best friends from college. They needed some fresh air and went for a walk, taking their cell phones along. Kristen tried to get her mother to come along, but Marcia said no, she didn't want to leave the house. There might be some news.

"Okay," Kristen said, trying again to reassure her mother. "Watch, you'll get a call when we're all outside."

It was still cool around noon, but the sun was out and the wind had subsided. Kristen had kept sending out mass text messages, asking for prayers for her brother, trying to sound upbeat, but she had been irked by some of the replies. "Why did they go out there?" some asked. It might have been a legitimate question, but now was not the time. Some of the questions were just ignorant: "Where are they?" If she knew where Nick and his friends were, she wouldn't be asking for prayers that they be found.

Five minutes after she left Nick's house, she got another message: "They just found a guy. Maybe that could be your brother."

Kristen's knees went weak. The message wasn't from someone whom she considered a reliable source. The person wasn't even in Tampa. But Kristen started running, crying, her legs giving out, trying to get back to the house as fast as she could.

As she ran, her father called.

"They found somebody," Stu Schuyler said. "It's Nick, they found Nick."

"Are you sure?" Kristen asked.

"It has to be," he said.

Kristen kept running. She got to the house and saw Paula outside.

"They found somebody," Kristen said.

Paula knew already. She told Kristen not to go inside. Her mother was a mess. She was falling apart.

Marcia Schuyler had learned of a rescue from Scott Miller, a friend of Nick's and Will's. He had rushed into the living room and said, "They found somebody, turn on Channel 9."

Marcia tried to change the channel, but she was a wreck and couldn't push the buttons on the remote control. Ben Busbee helped her and she saw a news crawl that said one person had been found alive, sitting on the boat.

"It's gotta be Nick!" she screamed, hopeful and crying.

Paula had been next door and had rushed over when she heard the scream. Busbee was holding Marcia up on the sofa. It seemed as if everyone had seen a ghost.

"What, what?" Paula yelled.

They told her that one person had been found alive. He was hanging on to the boat.

"No one lose hope," Paula said. "Everybody pray."

Paula called the Coast Guard station in St. Petersburg. Was it true? Was one man found?

Yes, it was true.

"Alive?"

"Yes."

Paula asked if the man had a tattoo on his back,

a Chinese symbol that meant "sky." That was Nick's nickname.

"I don't know, ma'am," the man at the Coast Guard station said.

They hung up. There was still no confirmed identity.

Marcia sat in the living room, crying, saying over and over, "It's gotta be Nick. If it's anybody, it would be Nick."

She felt bad for Scott Miller, who was a childhood friend of Will Bleakley's, but Nick was her son and she couldn't give up hope. Kristen hoped it was Nick, too, but one out of four had been found, the television said. There was only a 25 percent chance it would be her brother.

At the St. Petersburg Coast Guard station, Captain Timothy Close received a phone call from Stu Schuyler.

"I heard on the news you found somebody," Stu said. "Is it Nick?"

"Yes."

"Are you sure?"

"He's told us several times who he is, and we're going to believe him," Captain Close said.

Nick was on a Coast Guard cutter and would be airlifted to Tampa General Hospital. Stu Schuyler was at home in Tarpon Springs. His sister was with him. He hung up the phone and ran outside yelling. She chased after him.

"Is it good or bad?" his sister asked.

"Good," Stu said. "They found him."

Captain Close then phoned Marcia Schuyler and introduced himself. She got off the couch and walked through the kitchen to the deck of Nick's house.

"Did you find my son?" Marcia asked.

"Yes, ma'am, we did," he replied.

"It's Nick? Are you sure it's Nick?"

Marcia screamed, "They found Nick," then she passed out and dropped her cell phone.

"Hello? Hello?" Captain Close said on the other end.

Marcia awakened with a towel on her forehead. Kristen Schuyler called Captain Close back. Marcia got on the phone.

"I know he knows his name," she told Captain Close. "You have to make sure."

She feared that the survivor might be Will. He might be delirious and uttering Nick's name instead of his own. She couldn't bear to show up at the hospital or the Coast Guard station to greet Nick and walk in to find that it was Will. She felt guilty and selfish for thinking that way, but she was a mother who was desperate to find her son.

"We found your son," Captain Close assured her. "It's Nick."

Paula called the Coast Guard again, just to confirm it for herself. Yes, it was Nick. Everyone was hugging and crying and later Paula noticed that Scott Miller had gone outside. He had gone to high school with Will. One of Scott's friends, Nick, had been found, but Will had not been. Scott sat on his pickup, alone, his head down.

Marcia, Paula, and Kristen were driven to Tampa General Hospital, where they met with Stu. On the way, Stu got a call from a friend in Ohio, Bill Lally, who had been the best man at his wedding to Marcia. Bill was watching videotaped footage of the rescue. "I'm watching your son being lifted into a chopper as we speak," Bill said. "He looks fine."

"Are you sure it's Nick?" Stu asked.

"I've met Nick," Bill said. "I know what he looks like. It's Nick."

At the hospital, Stu rushed in so quickly that it felt as if he knocked the emergency room doors off their tracks. Marcia asked to see her son, the missing boater who had been found. Frantically, she decided to look for the helipad and began running down a hallway. A security guard stopped her.

"They just found my son," she said. "I need to get to him."

Just wait here a minute, the security guard said. He would find out where they had taken Nick. A few minutes later, a nurse appeared and said, "Come with me."

Marcia walked down a hallway into a room in Urgent Care and saw Nick lying on a bed, hooked up to intravenous tubes. It seemed as if a couple of doctors were on each side of him. It felt surreal to her. She was standing there, looking at her son, but she wasn't there at the same time.

She stood and watched for a minute or two, then began to make her way to Nick's side. She touched his hand. It felt cold. She bent down and kissed him and said, "God, Nick, you scared the hell out of me."

"I know, I know," he said.

He put his hand on top of his mother's. Marcia had tried to be strong, but now she was sobbing. Nick patted her hand, comforting her, as if to say, "It's okay, it's okay."

Marcia stood on his left side. Nick had his head turned. He opened his eyes and said, "Do you know what kept me going the whole time?"

Does he know who I am? Marcia wondered. Is he delirious? Does he think I'm Paula and he's about to say something I shouldn't hear?

"I wasn't going to let you go to my funeral," Nick said. "I knew it would kill you, Mom."

Marcia was crying and shaking. "I'm so proud of you," she told Nick. "I'm so glad you didn't give up."

She tried to hug her son, but someone in the room suggested she leave, saying it was urgent that they take care of Nick. On a tray, Marcia saw the cross that Nick had worn around his neck. She took it as she walked out.

Later, Marcia returned to see Nick, along with Paula, Kristen, and Stu. This time Nick was giving a statement to the Coast Guard and to an investigator from the Florida Wildlife and Fisheries Commission. His eyes were mostly closed. When he opened them, Paula noticed, they rolled back in his head. His lips were crusted with salt. She could hear the dryness in his voice.

"Hi, babe," she said. Nick grabbed her hand and told her he loved her. She wasn't crying, but she was nervous, both because of the officials in the room and because Nick's eyes would sometimes roll back.

"Kisses," Nick said, and Paula gave him a kiss.

They talked for a few minutes. He asked about the dogs. As Paula was leaving the room, Nick said, "Babe, come here."

"Closer," he said.

"I'm gonna marry you," Nick told Paula.

As she left the room, he waggled his right index finger. It was part of a goofy ritual that he performed when he was trying to be funny.

"Feeling pretty good," Nick said.

Kristen noticed that Nick had been bleeding. Struggling to keep his eyes open, he asked, "Who's in here?" Kristen said, "Hi, Nick," and kissed him. His skin was salty and his toes felt icy. He seemed thin, pale, dehydrated, and he struggled to talk. When investigators asked him about the other guys on the boat, he shook his head, saying they were all gone.

A few moments after Paula and Kristen left the room, there was a report on television, an unconfirmed report, that a second fisherman had been found, Marquis Cooper. For a moment, Kristen doubted her brother. Maybe he was hallucinating.

"Nick, they found Marquis," Kristen later told him.

"No, they didn't," he said.

"Nick, it's on the news."

"Kris, no," Nick said. "He died in my arms. They're not going to find him."

When Nick arrived at Tampa General, his body temperature had risen to 95 degrees. He seemed a bit confused, but otherwise "was not in that bad a condition," according to Dr. Mark Rumbak, the critical care specialist who examined him. There was some concern about damage to the muscles in his legs from the cold and from banging against the boat. His blood platelet count was also low.

"The whole of his lower limbs was one big bruise," Dr. Rumbak said. He had the hospital's vascular experts check to make sure that swelling in Nick's legs had not compromised the blood supply. As was common with patients in intensive care, Nicks' legs were fitted with a cufflike compression device to stimulate blood flow and to prevent clots from forming.

Nick's body temperature when found had been variously measured at 88.8 to 89.5 degrees. This is known as moderate hypothermia. Sometimes doctors purposely lower to this temperature the bodies of patients suffering from stroke, acute liver failure, cardiac arrest, or acute brain injury. It was a therapeutic measure that decreased the body's metabolism, reducing the need for oxygen.

Nick probably could have lived another six to twelve hours in the Gulf, Dr. Rumbak said. He was not quite at the point where he was nearing death. And because his temperature had risen steadily as he changed out of his wet clothes on the cutter *Tornado* and wrapped himself in wool blankets, there was no need to inject him with warm fluids at the hospital. His platelet count would rise to normal levels and the bruises would heal on his legs. Still, one issue defied any exact medical explanation: How had Nick survived when the others had not?

"I have no idea," Dr. Rumbak said. "These people were all very fit. They were basically the same age and the same size. I don't think most people would have survived this. I think it is a miracle in a way."

On the one hand, Nick had little body fat to provide insulation against the cold. On the other hand, as a personal trainer, he was terrifically fit.

"He is well built and doesn't have an ounce of fat," Dr. Rumbak said. "That was probably to his disadvantage. But then again, he was so fit. One thing about football players and professional athletes, generally, they push through their pain. They just don't stop. He's not only fit, he's got that mind-set that he's not giving up."

Perhaps his childhood in Ohio—wearing shorts when it was 25 degrees—had made him more acclimated to the cold than the others. And it could only have helped that Nick put on a sweatshirt and winter jacket once he became seasick.

"I think having this must have to some degree slowed down the loss of heat," Dr. Rumbak said. "It must have. It's so unusual that he would have survived so much longer than the other guys. They were all pretty much the same.

"It's amazing how we get prepared for something like that. Growing up near Cleveland, wearing shorts in the cold. He had been a football player. He's a personal trainer. He's used to going through adversity. He gets sick, so he puts on slightly warmer clothes than the other guys. In spite of that, I'm still surprised he got through it. I really am. That's amazing."

There was one other possible factor that contributed to his perseverance. "He kept saying that he didn't want his mother to go to his funeral," Dr. Rumbak said.

It was a misconception to think that Marquis, Corey, and Will had simply given up in the water, Dr. Rumbak said. Hypothermia can lead to delirium, along with a drop in potassium levels and a breakdown of the cell membranes in the heart until it can no longer contract, he said.

"They were just confused," Dr. Rumbak said. "You saw that in *Titanic*. They become confused and they slip away. You're shivering and you're so cold and eventually I think it gets into your brain and you become confused and then you just slip away. If Nick had tied them to the boat, their hearts probably would have stopped before they were found."

While survivor's guilt was real and could be tormenting, there was no reason for Nick to feel guilty, he said. "I think he's got a lot of demons now," Dr. Rumbak said. "He think it's his fault, and it's not. It's not his fault because he survived and they didn't. He didn't kill them. He didn't try to end their lives. It wasn't them or him. Their lives just happened to be shorter because they got colder quicker or whatever it was. And they would have died anyway, irrespective of what he did. I don't know if he can accept that. Hopefully, he will someday."

In the hospital, they poked me, shot me with needles, and injected blood thinners into my belly to prevent clots. I had an oxygen mask on. At one point I looked at my heart rate and it was in the 120s. They put a catheter in. A guy said, "It'll be over before you know it." It felt like they used a drill. Finally, they gave me something for my butt: Silvadene cream. The nurse said they used it for burn victims.

That first day I asked for a chicken sandwich and a Coke. By the time they brought it, I was sleeping. Later, I had the sandwich and a bit of lasagna and ice cream and Jell-O. The TV was on in my room in intensive care, and I saw myself getting off the helicopter. The same feelings of guilt and sadness came back. I got upset and shook my head; I changed the channel to another station. I was interested, but a lot of the things they reported were not right. They were saying the search continues and it's not looking good for the other three guys. I kept shaking my head. "They're gone," I said.

Not that they were wasting their time with the search, but I knew nobody would find them.

"They're gone."

I was a little overwhelmed. I wanted as many people as possible in my room. I had been alone so long, and now I wanted to be around the people I thought I'd never see again. I felt guilty. Why was I the one on the boat who was found? They should have been working on Will next to me. He should have been in the same room in the ICU. There wasn't a moment I didn't think he wouldn't make it until a couple of hours before he passed.

The doctor came in to check my blood pressure. I was shaking my head. "What's wrong?" the nurse asked.

"They're gone," I said.

"It'll be okay," she said.

I began to feel a little warmer. A few friends came by. Scott Miller was there. He was Will's other best friend. They had grown up together and had been roommates in college. I told him the story quickly. He had to go tell Will's family right after that. I felt bad for Scott. There were people so excited I had made it through, but there was a melancholy feeling, too. Scott was my friend, but Will was his best friend. One had been saved, the other was lost.

I told the story to Ben Busbee, who still played tight end at USF. He had been there with my mother when she got the call that I had been found. Paula sat there in the room, listening. I looked over and everyone was staring at me. I felt frail and thin. I looked at my arms. They had atrophied, like after you have surgery. They were so puny. I was upset. Everything I worked for physically was gone. My wrists felt as thick as my biceps.

I kept flipping channels. My eyes started watering. I had mixed feelings. I'd watch the TV reports, down and upset with everything going through my mind. But I would look around and feel good. My family and Paula and my close friends were there supporting me. Unfortunately, my closest friend wasn't there, the one I really wanted with me.

I drank tons of water. The first time I peed, I had the catheter in. It burned like someone had taken a lighter to me. My urine was dark yellow from the dehydration. A doctor came in and moved my legs around. I had bad bruises all over my legs. My ankles were twice their normal size. They were worried about my knees and whether I had torn any ligaments. I told them, no, they were just sore from banging on the boat. They worked my legs, and I kept saying, "Whoa!" My butt hurt so bad.

The second day in the hospital, I kept watching TV. I'd see pictures of boats and helicopters. I knew they wouldn't find anybody. I had thick socks on. My legs were swollen and hard. They put something on me, like a heating pad, to increase the blood flow in my legs. It was too tight. My legs were so tender, I didn't want anybody touching anything.

Two guys from the Florida Wildlife and Fisheries Commission came to my room. I told them the story over about forty-five minutes. It was very hard. Later, I ate ice cream, Jell-O, pulled pork, rice, subs, four kinds of pasta, anything I wanted. My butt was still raw. The back of my gown was open and I bled through the sheets. It took a few people to roll me onto another bed, and there was just raw burning pain, like I was sitting on a blowtorch. A week later, I would pull off scabs that were four inches long.

I felt heavy, obese, like I couldn't move anything. But I wanted people around me. I didn't want to talk, I just wanted to listen. I was grateful to see others, to smell something other than myself or salt water. I was even grateful for the different pains I felt. Needles made me feel alive.

I spoke to Will's parents. I was dreading it, but I was the only one who knew the story. I had to tell them what had happened to their son. I told them how sorry I was. The first few minutes, it was very tough. They asked, what happened? I told them, without going into full details. They asked if the guys were drinking. I said yes, but that wasn't the reason this happened. They questioned a couple of our choices—putting the anchor line at the back of the boat was the main one. I'm pretty sure it was Will's dad who said, "Will knows better than that. He's taken boating safety classes." I don't think he wanted to believe me. I wouldn't have wanted to believe me, either.

It was a twenty-minute conversation. There was a lot of quiet time. I asked, "Are you there?" Everyone was in shock.

It was the same feeling I felt when I got into that motorcycle wreck in high school and had to face Daniel Turner's parents. It was something that absolutely had to be done, but I was so scared. I felt defenseless and helpless. I really did all I could to help their son survive. I really did. I told them Will did everything he could to help me and without him, no way in hell I would be having this conversation with them now, not without his going under the boat to get the life jackets, Gatorade, and pretzels, not without working together.

That was the most difficult phone call I ever made. I sat there by myself for a good five minutes, knowing there was no good or correct way to say it. Will's parents mentioned a funeral, a memorial. His mom said she thought it was best to have it as soon as possible. That was the last thing I wanted to think about. But I realized my best friend's parents had lost their youngest son. I knew it was awful for them. Nothing would be able to console them.

Late that Tuesday night, around midnight, they took X-rays of my feet, knees, and ankles. My legs were swollen and stiff; the range of motion was gone. My hip and groin felt completely destroyed from holding Marquis, like I had worked out continuously for a couple of days. There was no strength or flexibility left.

I also began experiencing bad heartburn. It was getting hard to breathe. I was taking Pepcid AC, Maalox, and Tums, and they gave me an IV for heartburn, but it kept getting worse and worse. The next morning, the doctor explained that the medicine, inactivity, and the intake of salt water was causing this feeling. The more I sat up, the worse it got. I gasped for air. After a while, they gave me oxygen. It felt like someone was taking his hands and squeezing my heart. I kept telling Paula, "I can't breathe. I feel like I'm having a heart attack."

That day, the Wildlife and Fisheries Commission issued a small statement. I don't know if what I said wasn't clear to them, or if everything got flipped around in the media. There were reports that Marquis just gave up and died. There were reports that we were drunk, that that's why the boat flipped. Reports that we had been fighting with one another, that Corey had gotten aggressive, punching Will and throwing punches at me, and that he took his life jacket off and gave up. Reports that Will had swum off on his own toward a light. If I told anybody this, they misinterpreted it, or I misspoke, because I was incoherent at times right after I was rescued. I'm the one who saw the light and nearly swam to it, not Will.

These inaccurate rumors were driving me crazy. I felt it was disrespectful. I don't know anybody else who would have made it that long through those conditions like Marquis, Corey, and Will did. I didn't know anyone else who could have survived as long as they did. I got lucky; I had more clothing.

The nurse said, "We're going to get you on your feet today." I got up and it was like walking on Play-Doh. I felt an extra inch of padding on my feet. They were soft and doughy. Pain shot through my legs and butt. I felt light-headed, and after thirty seconds, they had to put me in a chair next to the bed. I was glad, though. At least I could feel my legs. On the boat my feet had gotten so cold and numb that I thought there was a good chance I would lose them.

My heartburn kept getting worse. They were giving me Tums, Maalox, Mylanta—but it wasn't getting better. Maybe going to the bathroom would help. The nurse helped me out of bed. I went in a portable toilet, and they had baby wipes there. I thought I had been in the most pain on the boat, but I was wrong. These wipes made the little match I felt in my butt turn into a bonfire, like someone had lit a stick of dynamite. I screamed.

They also got concerned about the MRSA bacteria, which is resistant to all kinds of penicillin. It lives in your nose and on your skin and is usually harmless. But if you have a lot of cuts and scrapes like I did, it could cause a serious staph infection. My immune system was down, so they were worried. Everyone in the room had to put on a gown, gloves, and a mask.

I saw on TV that Marquis's dad asked for planes and boats to conduct a volunteer private search. I didn't want to say anything, but I knew it was a waste of time. I understood what he was doing. He was a father, and he didn't want to give up on finding his son. I thought it was amazing that he would do that and that people would donate their time and money. But I knew they would never find Marquis's body, not alive anyway, unless they had a scuba team or a submarine.

Thursday came, my fourth day in the hospital. My heartburn was still constant, but it was getting better. The doctor said my kidneys were much improved. There was a chance I could go home today. They did more tests, and finally I told the nurse, "That's it. You've taken my blood a hundred times. You've stuck me with enough needles. You can take the IVs out."

They wouldn't let me out, though, unless I could walk a lap around the ICU. It was very weird standing on my feet. I was wobbling, walking like an old lady. It took me a couple of minutes, but I made it around the ICU. I leaned on the counter and signed the dismissal papers. We knew that most of the media were out front, so we sneaked out the back.

It felt so good to be home and out of the hospital. Paula never left my side, which was very comforting. I stood next to the car for ten minutes, trying to delay the inevitable of walking up the stairs to the living room. It took awhile, but I made it. The dogs let out barks and cries and started licking me. It was a really good feeling, like being greeted by your children.

After I got home, I weighed myself. I had gone from 240 to 208. I was used to eating 5,000 calories a day. Then I went for two days eating nothing on the boat. In the hospital, I ate the entire supply of sugar-free Jell-O in the ICU. Paula went to the grocery store the next day and overheard a woman say, "My mother's in ICU at Tampa General and there's no Jell-O on the whole floor." It was because of me. They treated me like a king there, but I was still losing weight.

It was a Friday now, and Will's funeral was the next day. I dreaded going. I knew how difficult it would be. The thought of it put everything into perspective. It was real now. He was really gone.

I knew that day, like the accident, I would never forget. Going to a best friend's memorial, especially at my age, was something I definitely didn't know how to handle or had ever experienced before. On Saturday morning, Paula, my mom, my sister, and I drove an hour north from Tampa to Crystal River. No one said much in the car. I cried the whole way. It was hard on Paula, too. Will was also her best friend.

I was really nervous. We were going to meet the families of Marquis, Corey, and Will. I didn't know how the meeting would go or what I would say. I wasn't walking well, either. How long would I be able to stand?

I knew a lot of people had different questions and opinions about what had happened. Did I survive by killing those three guys? That was absurd. Everything I had told the Coast Guard and the Wildlife and Fisheries Commission was true, but there was no way to prove any of it. I could see how disgusting it would be if somebody got away with doing harm to their friends.

Before the memorial, we all met at Scott Miller's house. It had become a worldwide story. Even Paula's family in Brazil had heard about it. So we went to Scott's, trying to dodge the media. We passed the church on the way and there was a sign that said, WE LOVE YOU WILL BLEAKLEY. It had his birthday and the day he passed. As soon as I saw that sign, I lost it again.

At Scott's we met all the families—fathers, mothers, sisters, brothers, cousins. There were probably twenty-five of us. I was very nervous and sad. Everyone was crying. I kind of limped out of the car. Scott was one of the first to come up to me. He gave me a big hug. I met Corey's sisters and hugged Rebekah, Marquis's wife. Marquis's mother cried on my shoulder. I think it was his mom who said, "Thanks for being there for my baby." A couple families said, "Thanks for hanging on and for being here and being able to tell the story."

It was difficult hugging Will's parents. They knew I was the last one with their son. It was so sad. No matter what I said, it wouldn't make any of these families feel better or smile. It was an awful way to meet someone.

The meeting probably went on for ten minutes. We were all outside at this point, in Scott's parents' driveway. Marquis's father, Bruce, hung back a little. He's a sportscaster in Phoenix, and he had a million questions. He kind of wanted to hear details of things that hadn't been said yet. How had the boat flipped? Why did we tie the anchor line to the back? Had we been drinking? He wanted to know the whole ordeal of Marquis getting sick, how he had died. I was caught off guard a little. These were a lot of questions that there was no good way to answer. It was hard to speak to him. He had so much of Marquis in his face. I'd answer, and he'd have a rebuttal. I was more mentally exhausted than I had been all week. I wasn't quite prepared. Had it been anybody else, I wouldn't have done it. Especially at that time and place. But I had held on to his son, and his son had died in my arms. I knew he deserved answers, and I tried to give them as thoroughly as I could.

As we got out of the car at the church, I noticed that people were staring at me, curious. It was the first time I had been in public. I was at the center of attention when it should have been all about Will. No one knows how to deal with that at their best friend's funeral. We went into a chorus room and met Will's aunts, uncles, cousins, and close friends who had grown up with him.

We stood there and shook people's hands. Some thanked me for holding on, for being with Will to the end. I started getting the same nauseous feeling I had on the boat when I got seasick. I couldn't believe I was going to my best friend's funeral—my best friend who had died in my arms. I wasn't able to save him. This could have been my funeral just as easily. I wasn't more than a few hours from being in the same position he had been in, from having the same thing happen to me.

At the front of the church they had big pictures of Will, his baseball and football jerseys from high school, and his football jersey from USF. There were flowers and pictures of him at graduation. I lost it again. I can't believe I'm at this frickin' funeral, I thought to myself. I really did lose my friend.

Will had done everything he could to prolong my life. We had worked together. I was still alive and attending his funeral because of him. He helped keep me alive. There easily could have been four funerals instead of three. I owed my life partially to Will. I had sent his parents a bouquet of flowers. On the card, I wrote, "To the family of the angel that saved my life. He will never be forgotten."

For most of the ceremony, I thought about Will and his last hours. Will's brother said some nice things about him. One of his cousins sang a song by Sarah McLachlan, "Angel." She had a beautiful voice. As soon as the piano started, I got hysterical. I don't think I had ever cried that hard. I wanted to scream or hit something. I felt sad, upset, frustrated, angry, and guilty. I started thinking, Could I have done something different? Could I have done a better job of giving Will CPR? Should I have given my jacket to him for a while? If I did that, would he have lived a little longer and I would have eventually died? Should I have helped him go underneath the boat?

Reverend David Lane, the football reverend at USF, was at the service. He had visited me in the hospital. When the funeral was over, the reverend was at the front of the church, at the altar, next to a picture of Will. I stopped and stared at Will. I could barely see. I hugged the reverend and squeezed as hard as I could. I cried on his shoulder. The three of us had prayed together before. Through him, I felt a spiritual connection to Will.

After the memorial, we went outside to a pavilion to have a meal. I had knots in my stomach. I was waddling along. The media was there. I could see TV cameras focused on me. I could hear the clicking of cameras. I was annoyed. Did they have to do that now?

We had a nice meal. People couldn't have been nicer to me. A lot of friends and former teammates, even guys from Ohio who knew Will, came in for the memorial. I know everyone had questions, but they knew it wasn't the right time. They were very respectful. But other than having three friends die in my arms, this was the worst day I had experienced. It reminded me of the accident. Every time I thought something couldn't get worse, it did. I lost one friend, then two, then three. It always got worse. Then I heard Will's cousin sing that song. I knew, okay, it can't get any worse than right now. I'll never forget that song and the way she sang it and the way I felt for those four minutes. I knew this was as bad as it was going to get.

Epilogue

The first few days home from the hospital, I got lots of rest. I was physically and mentally exhausted. Shell-shocked. Then I got restless. I'd toss and turn and look at the clock. It would be one o'clock in the morning, then two o'clock, then three. For a while, I got only a few hours of sleep. Night was always the worst. It still kind of happens now. I don't have nightmares, but things go through my head: Why am I here? Why am I the only who got through this? Because I happened to get seasick and put on more clothes? That sucks. It's not fair.

For a month, when I tried to sleep everything ran through my mind, particularly the last few moments with each guy. I pictured the water and the waves and the sound the wind made, the taste I had in my mouth, that bitter, dry taste.

I kept picturing their faces when I lost them. Marquis was gone and I held him tight to my body. He foamed at the mouth and I kept wiping the foam away. His eyes were shut, his body was dead-weight, and I held him even though I knew he was gone.

I kept picturing Corey, that mean, growling face, those big eyes, the things he said. It hurts to this day, though I know Corey in his right mind would never say anything like that.

I kept picturing the sad look that Will had, the way he bear-hugged me from behind on the boat and the tone in his voice when he said he wouldn't make it through another night, when he said he loved me, when he said how hungry and thirsty and cold he was, that sad, crying, dying voice.

I took three weeks off from work, then I kind of got sick of laying around. I felt better physically, so I went into the gym a few hours a day. I was down thirty pounds. I felt like garbage.

Before, I could bench-press 400 pounds. Now I could barely lift 135. I was so atrophied and weak. I had no muscular endurance. It took awhile to get it back. In my mind, I wanted to go for it, but I had to be patient. A few days, I did too much and got sore like I had never worked out before. My legs and groin were so weak, I couldn't do a lunge. My flexibility was shot. I couldn't touch my ankles, my lower back was so tight. I could barely reach below my knees. It would take me three months to put the weight back on. I've got my strength back, but eight months later, I'm still not in the same shape.

It was a bittersweet feeling going back to work. I got back in the swing of things, but I was a little overwhelmed. The media knocked on my door, contacted my friends, followed me to lunch. At the gym, people were so nice. Everyone was coming up and hugging me and saying, "Thanks for holding on, you're such an inspiration." People sent food and flowers and hundreds of cards—anonymous people, friends from Tampa, and parents of people I had grown up with in Ohio. It felt good. I'll never forget it.

I got a big envelope from third-graders in Utah. They were learning a new word every week about values. The word for the week they wrote to me was "determined." They probably sent thirty letters and drawings, in the blunt, cute, innocent way that kids have: "I'm so sorry that your friends drowned. I love fish. What's your favorite color?" It was sweet. I broke down and cried.

I appreciated everything, but it was a bit much. It felt good—and it didn't feel good. I wasn't able to save anybody. If only at least one more of us could have made it. I wished we had never gone fishing that day or that we had gone in the summer when the water wouldn't have been cold or that there wouldn't have been a storm that night. So many ifs, ifs, ifs.

Paula Oliveira: When Nick got back from hospital, he told me the story again, with more details. For the first few weeks, I thought, Wow, he's doing well. Then it just hit him one day. Nick is usually the life of the party, always ready with a good comeback. We laugh a lot. He went from that to totally withdrawn, silent, mute. He didn't want to talk about anything. That was scary to me.

There was complete silence in the house. We went a long time with no laughter. I could be sitting in the same room, and I felt alone. He'd come home sometimes and he'd sit in his truck for a few minutes and he would come in and his eyes were bloodshot. He'd sit on the couch and just sob.

I had lost my best friend, too, in Will. I felt like I couldn't mourn in my own house. If Nick wasn't thinking about it, I didn't want to bring it up.

Our conversations would be surface. How was your day? What do you want for dinner? How are the dogs? If the conversation got too deep or related to the accident, he would completely shut down.

For a while, I stopped making the attempt.

He would sit there and say, "Why me?" Over and over, I don't know how many times.

He never showed me any signs that he might hurt himself. But he really got to a dark place. There were no warning signs. The person he was and the person he became changed so quickly. It was terrifying. It broke me. I felt that nothing I said was right. I'm a teacher. I was home for the summer. It was the summer of hell. He wasn't angry, he was sad. He'd have to be up early for work, and I would make him an awesome breakfast, thinking this might start his day on the right foot. I tried anything to lighten the mood. I would do anything for him. And he would just say, "Thanks, babe." I never got thanks-babed so much. I knew he was grateful, but he didn't have it in him at the time.

I didn't want to take it personally, but it was a hard time.

I asked him if he felt guilty, and he said that was the one thing he didn't feel. He knew he did everything he could have done at the time. But he was distraught. Out of the blue, he would say, "I just don't get why I'm still here." Nothing would trigger it. He'd just say something like, "I think about it all the time."

The forty-three hours that he was in the water and the aftermath were both hell for me, but to be honest, I think the aftermath was worse. Six months after the accident, his mood finally brightened. Slowly, he came back to himself. He had more to say to me. He could laugh again. He's good with comebacks, and the sarcastic smartass part of him came back. I think all this changed me. If I can get through this, I feel I can do anything.

I knew right away, even in the hospital, that I was going to get a tattoo. I knew it would have the guys' names or initials, something that tied the four of us together. I knew this would stay with me as long as I lived. And I knew they would stay with me. The four of us had worked together, and because of that I was still alive.

I looked through some quotes in a book that someone sent me. I found one from a Persian proverb that said, "In the hour of adversity, be not without hope." I thought, Okay, that's it, that's the one. Nothing more needs to be said. There was no giving up, no quitting. We worked together. Never once did we say, "We're done."

An artist friend came up with the design, a Celtic cross with their initials on each point of the cross. Victor Marquis Cooper, William Ward Bleakley, Corey Dominic Smith. It's on my right triceps, with the quote in the background and a date at the bottom, 3/1/2009, the day they died. There is a rope intertwined with the cross and an anchor at the bottom. Funny how 31 was my basketball number in high school. And how I meant the cross to be a symbol for the will to survive, and Will was the name of my best friend. Go figure.

My arm was so atrophied that I had to wait three months to build it up before I got the tattoo. Paula had a small anchor tattooed on her ribs, to honor Will. When I got the tattoo, the artist said, "Are you ready?" and I thought, I could do this all day. I had a different level of pain tolerance now. I almost dozed off. I'd rather go through the pain of a tattoo a million times than go through what I did in the water, losing my friends.

I made my tattoo into my profile photo on Facebook. I started getting criticized because I still hadn't spoken to the media. Some people wrote nice tributes. Others said, "Isn't it time to talk?" Everyone was giving me advice. I knew I could never please everybody, no matter what I did. The only thing that mattered to me was the guys' families. Everyone had their own way of dealing with it. Some bloggers were just brutal: I can't believe he got a tattoo. He probably killed those three guys. This shows how weak "niggers" are; they can't even hold on to a boat. Just the lowest, most absurd and vile things. I knew better. I shouldn't have read the blogs. I didn't think it was important to set the record straight publicly. I was annoyed with the media. I wasn't ready to talk yet. I just wanted to get back to my regular lifestyle and move forward.

SHORTLY AFTER I got my tattoo, Rebekah Cooper had a memorial for Marquis. It was a Saturday in the summer. Corey's and Will's families attended. I went with Paula, my mom, my dad, and my sister. About seventy people showed up for the service at a church in Tampa. Some of his former teammates were there, and some of his local friends. I woke up that morning and I was nervous. In a way it was selfish. I hadn't broken down in a while. I knew this was going to be hard. But it wasn't going to be as hard on me as it would be for Rebekah and Delaney and Marquis's mom. Even though Delaney understood that her dad was gone and was in heaven and was always watching, she would never have her father again. She would have to grow up without him. It saddened me.

Someone had written a song about Delaney and Marquis smiling down on her. During the service, the reverend asked people to raise their hands if they had learned anything from Marquis. Somebody said, "He gave me the okay to laugh." Another person stood up and told a funny story about being on the team with him. Some said things that were more serious than others. I knew I had to say something or I'd regret it later. I was the last one. I raised my hand and, half-crying, I said, "Marquis taught me to never give up and never quit."

Rebekah had a speech written. She talked about how they met and what a good husband and father Marquis had been. The three of them had a motto: together they were one heartbeat. Rebekah was very emotional. It killed me to see her like that. She talked about how Marquis said she was his anchor. And that if he ever went out, this was the way he would have wanted, fishing on the water, and now he was in God's hands and his spirit was with us today. I can't imagine how she got through it. I had tears dripping on the floor.

A FEW DAYS after the service, I talked to Corey's two sisters and his brother. It was gut-wrenching. Here was another family to which I had to explain what their brother went through in the last few hours of his life. It was hard. Part of me wanted to leave out the part about him being aggressive and losing it. It wasn't him. He was suffering from hypothermia. But I didn't leave it out. I felt honesty was the best thing. Coming from me, it would have meant a lot more to them than hearing it from somebody else.

I spoke about how we went into the water and fought for one another. Without Corey and Marquis and Will, I told them, I don't think I'd be here today. It was extremely difficult to explain how Corey went out, getting away from me, and my losing grip of his life jacket and seeing the look in his eyes and the last few words he said to me—"I'm a kill you"—and taking off his jacket and diving to the ocean floor. As soon as I told them that part, the three of them said, "No, no, no," like Corey wouldn't have said that. They knew it wasn't Corey. I told them that he was so easy to get along with, he was the nicest guy. He had never quit on anything. Fortunately, they understood what he had gone through. That wasn't the Corey we knew. It was the elements that made him do what he did. It was sad. We were all crying. They were breaking down to hear how their brother had died.

I wasn't able to save him. I'm the lone survivor. That's a pretty shitty, guilty feeling. I always pictured it the other way around, Will or Corey or Marquis surviving and having this conversation with my family. I felt so bad, so guilty, not for myself, but for the families. There was nothing I could do. I couldn't bring those guys back. I felt so sad for their families. I knew how I felt about my mother when I was on the boat, and now the other three families had to go through that.

ONCE THINGS CALMED down, I reached out and got Rebekah to hang out with Paula a bit. They went to a movie from time to time, or to dinner, just to get away. I knew she had been so busy, taking care of her family and Marquis's family and her daughter, figuring out where to live.

I always felt there was going to be a natural connection with Rebekah and Delaney. I was always going to be tied to Marquis, the way he died in my arms and the final things he said about his family, how much he loved them, and how I kept yelling, "For your daughter, be strong for Goose and for Beck."

I babysat for Delaney a couple times, or she and her mom and Paula and I just hung out. I loved hanging out with Delaney. I took her to Chuck E. Cheese's to build a stuffed animal. She picked a pink unicorn. A sound chip came with it, and they put her in this closet so she could create her own message. She said, "I love you, Mommy, I love you, Daddy," and we slipped the sound chip inside the unicorn. Every time you grabbed its foot, it would talk.

Paula and Rebekah had gone to a movie. When they got home, Delaney would press the foot and it would activate the sound and she would laugh hysterically at hearing her own voice. The first time Rebekah heard it, she choked up. Her eyes watered.

Eventually, we drifted apart. I told my story to HBO's *Real Sports* in August. I got permission from all the other families beforehand. Afterward, Rebekah said she needed time to herself and to mourn. Maybe the story was too graphic for her. Maybe she thought I was capitalizing on tragedy. I hope not. I just thought it was time for me to tell my story, to set the record straight. There were so many false rumors out there. The next day, I tried to contact some of the families. People had been texting me, thanking me for clearing up the record. I felt a little weight had been lifted off my shoulders.

Then I realized I hadn't spoken to Rebekah for a couple of weeks. She decided she wanted to distance herself from any type of media. She wanted some space and time to mourn. I respected that. But it was also hard to hear. I knew I wouldn't see her and Delaney as much as I had hoped.

We haven't been close since. The most important thing for me is what the families think and how they are dealing with their loss. People have to be allowed to grieve in their own way. Everyone has been so supportive of me, asking me how I'm doing, even though they are the ones who lost someone. I do care about Rebekah and Delaney. I think about them a couple times a day. I keep a picture of Delaney and me at Chuck E. Cheese's on the fridge. I still have a coloring book we had colored in on the table in the living room. I genuinely enjoyed hanging out with her. I wanted her to step out of the box and just let her be herself.

I respect any decisions the families make. At the same time, I feel like no matter whether we like it or what our feelings are, I'm always going to be connected to the families of Marquis, Corey, and Will. Even if we haven't talked in five years, I'll still feel that way, only I hope it's not like that. I hope they don't think, Oh, he's only trying to contact us because of what happened or out of pity. That's absolutely not true. Even though Marquis and I knew each other closely only a few months, we created a different relationship than I had with anyone else. It was more work than play, but I had nothing but respect for him. I looked up to him. I can't say that about a lot of people in my life at this stage.

I'm not going to give up. I hope I can be part of Rebekah and Delaney's lives. One of the things I learned from Marquis is that family and relationships meant the most to him. He always said that he and Rebekah had one heartbeat and she was his anchor.

I STARTED THE Nick Schuyler Foundation, which will host an annual flag-football tournament and other activities, to raise money for the Corey Smith Child Development Center, the Will Bleakley Scholarship Fund, the Coast Guard Foundation, and other charities.

Marcia Schuyler: I probably still go to bed every night crying. None of us are religious, but I pray every night and every morning, "Thank you, God, for saving my son. Please watch over him and my daughter." I hope all of the others are together up there.

I think the toughest thing for Nick ever was to let go of Will. He asked Will to go on the trip. I think that's going to eat at him forever.

Nick trains a little girl, Samantha, who is ten and has had an unfortunate life. She's beaten leukemia, she has osteoporosis, and she's had a stroke. She's a little overweight. She's a sweet girl, and she's been through a lot already. Understandably, she's been babied under the circumstances. When something hurts, her immediate reaction is "I quit." Nick tries to teach her that it's okay to hurt, to work through your pain threshold. He comes up with little games to get her to exercise: Nick Says instead of Simon Says. He trains her at a little playground at her community pool. They play tag and follow the leader, and he's made a little obstacle course. She has three dances, the hoedown—throw down, the ice-cream freeze, and break it down. She gets tired, things hurt on her body, and she wants to stop, but Nick keeps her moving: Slow it down, take a sec, don't quit. He tells her never to use the word *can't*.

The tips of both of my big toes are still numb. It's weird. I'll randomly stub my toe and think it's gonna hurt, but it doesn't. My hip flexor and my groin on the right side are not quite the same. My right foot, from holding Marquis, wants to turn out. It's not painful, but it's annoying. My hip feels like it needs to crack and pop. I go to the chiropractor once a week. It's tolerable, though. Every time I think of the accident, I know it could have been a lot worse.

I have a raised scar on my right foot and on one of the toes on my left foot from clinging to the underside of the boat. There is another scar on my calf, shaped like a cloud. The skin on my butt is still a little pink, but it has basically healed. My stomach has gotten better. For a while, I was either fine or I was starving. There was no in-between. Same thing with urinating. Either I'd be fine or I had to go right away. It was awful for a while. I felt like I was going to pee in my pants. Now it's getting better. The doctor says maybe the muscle in my bladder goes into spasms. There is medicine for it. Maybe I should get it looked at.

Psychologically, it's been a rough time. I'm back to my normal lifestyle, working full-time, trying to play basketball once a week and flag football on Saturdays. I try to have a life on the weekends. Some days are better than others. It's definitely not the same without Will, my wingman. I lived in Ohio until I was twenty or so, and when I came down to Tampa, he became one of my true friends, my best friend, here. To lose him and still live here, that's hard to cope with.

On the other hand, I know every day is a blessing that I'm here. Every morning, I see this tattoo, and it reminds me how lucky I am to be here and how easily I could be gone. I'm lucky I had those three guys with me. I'm lucky Will went under the boat and got those life jackets. That he went under and got me Gatorade and pretzels. I'm lucky I got sick and had all my clothes on, unlike everyone else. I'm even lucky Marquis bought that boat, because it is virtually unsinkable.

I've gotten so many e-mails and calls and text messages, saying, "God has a plan for you, stay strong, you may not see it now." I kind of see it both ways. I hope so, but why didn't God have a plan for these guys, as good as they were? Why did He choose me out of the four?

Especially at first, I was angry. How could this happen to me? Am I this bad person? I don't do drugs and steal. Why did it happen to Marquis and Corey and Will? They didn't do those things, either. I keep seeing the same images of the guys and their last few minutes, their faces, and the things they said. That will stick with me for the rest of my life.

Everyone was so nice to me, but I worry that the other families will have a bit of hatred for me, or resentment, or whatever the word is. It was nothing they did or said, but I could see how they might say, "How the hell did you live, and my son or brother or husband didn't?"

Sometimes I have dark moments. I'm selfish or feel sorry for myself or I get frustrated when things don't go my way and lose my temper and blow up, and I say things like, "That's God's way of showing me I shouldn't have made it through this," or "I should have gone down with my friends," or "Maybe I shouldn't have lived." I'll catch myself, or Paula will be around and say, "I can't believe you said that." That brings me back to reality.

I never thought about hurting myself. I never became suicidal. A lot of people say, "Are you seeing anyone? You should get help." I've just never been a person to sit and tell someone my feelings, especially a stranger. I know a psychiatrist or a psychologist is a professional and would want to help and is there to listen, but I know no matter what they say, you can't put yourself in that water and know how I loved these guys and how they died in my arms. I don't see the positive aspect of sitting there and explaining myself to somebody. When people, my friends, asked me questions about the accident, I was fine talking about it. I felt I could trust them. They were just curious. To go and talk to a complete stranger, that was something I didn't think was necessary. When my parents were divorced, I didn't talk about it much. I've always kept my feelings reserved. When things go wrong, I lean toward going to the gym and working out.

After the accident, I focused on getting back in shape, taking out my stress and anger on the weights. It was hard at first. It still is. I had such grueling workouts with Marquis and Corey. It was exciting to be with them in the gym. We pushed one another. It could be hard, and sometimes you felt like you wanted to puke, but I felt such a sense of enjoyment and accomplishment. I've worked with people since, but it hasn't had the same intensity. With them, I wanted to show off, to show that I was stronger and in better shape in so many aspects. It never felt like a job. With us, it was always, "Let's do a couple more sets of this or that." I switched gyms, not because I couldn't go back, but because it was a more realistic way to run my career. But I definitely miss working with Corey and Marquis. I haven't been able to push myself the same way. I don't know if I'll ever get that intensity or passion back.

An investigation by the Florida Fish and Wildlife Conservation Commission concluded that the accident was caused by three factors: improper tying of the anchor line to an eye bracket on the port side of the boat's transom; attempting to throttle forward to pull the anchor free; and failure to leave enough slack in the line, which led the stern to submerge and the boat to capsize.

Looking back, there are quite a few things I wish we had done differently. The anchor situation, of course. I wish I hadn't been as sick as I was. Maybe I would have been clearheaded enough to realize it was wrong to put the anchor line in the back of the boat. I didn't think much about it at the time. It sounded like a good idea. It never went through my head that something like this could happen, that it would be the last time that Marquis and Corey would see the sun. How could this twenty-one-foot boat, weighing more than three thousand pounds, with four big-ass dudes and a load of fish, get pulled down by an inch-thick anchor rope?

We should have been better prepared to send a distress signal, even if it was only because the engine might shut down or we might run out of gas. We should have told people the exact location where we were going. We should have been better equipped with flares and flashlights. We should have been wearing life jackets on the boat or had a better idea of where they were stored.

It's hard not to think, What if I had done this? What if I had done that? I was cold, but Will was obviously colder. What if I had let him wear my winter jacket? Or let him put my sweatshirt on? Maybe he would have lived longer. Or maybe it would have been a bad idea and he would have lived for a little while and I would have died, too. Who knows?

I wish I had found that steering cable earlier. Maybe I could have tied us together and we could have held on, all four of us. So many what-ifs.

We did some things wrong, but once we were in the water, we did a lot right. We did anything and everything that could have been done. We stuck together. We got life jackets from under the boat. If one fell off the boat, the others worked to grab him. We communicated well. We tried to right the boat and use our cell phones. We fought. No one gave up. Everyone gave everything they had until their last breath.

Three weeks after the accident, the Detroit Lions announced that for the 2009 season no one would wear number 93, the number that Corey Smith had worn for the team. His teammates talked about the relentless way Smith played. "If you could see the way this man worked," Galen Duncan, the Lions' player development director, told the Associated Press.

On October 18, 2009, the Oakland Raiders won an unlikely victory over the Philadelphia Eagles. During the game, a pigeon lined up with the Raiders' kickoff coverage team and flew downfield in formation with the players. Later, several of the Raiders told reporters that they believed the pigeon represented the spirit of Marquis Cooper. Even his mother, Donna Cooper, told one of her son's teammates, "That was Marquis out there with you guys."

On November 22, 2009, the Raiders dedicated a victory over the Cincinnati Bengals to Marquis. Rebekah and Delaney attended the game and were presented with a game ball. Beforehand, Delaney seemed excited, linebacker Sam Williams told reporters, saying, "She said, 'I get to see my daddy play!' Man. I spread the word and everybody felt the emotions. It was special."

A month after the accident, the Cleveland Cavaliers hooked me up with tickets when they came to play in Orlando. I finally got to meet LeBron James. He was a nice, humble guy. He asked how my mother was doing. Very sincere, very nice. First thing he said to me was, "I thought *I* was blessed."

I TRY TO abide by the fortune-cookie phrases, to cherish every day and don't take anything for granted. I try to move on, but it's always in the back of my mind, the same questions. At the end of each month, they always come, like another bill to be paid. A month passes and I think about how I've tried to deal with it, and I keep reminding myself that I could be gone and Will could be here. Why did I live and the other three die? How are their families doing? Will's parents lost a son; Rebekah lost a husband and the father of her daughter; Corey's family lost a brother and a son— they lost blood. They were my friends, my best friend, but I didn't lose blood.

Even now, I'll be planning a weekend, or some other activity, and I'll still think, Okay, I'll call Will, or Let's see what Will's doing. And then I catch myself. Or I'll call a person Will because I'm always thinking about him, seeing him in someone else's face. When I watch TV, I think, Will used to sit on the couch where I'm sitting. When Paula and I go out, I think, Last New Year's, we were with Will. Last Halloween, we were with Will. People ask me when I'm going to go camping again, and I wonder, Can I do this again without Will? It's never going to be the same.

Since the accident, I've been to the beach, but not in the water. Last Memorial Day weekend, we went to Indian Rocks Beach, off of St. Pete Beach. We played beach volleyball. I put my foot in the water and told Kristen, "It's about thirty degrees warmer than the last time I felt it." I stared at the water. I didn't want to go in—it made me sick to my stomach. Before, I would have jumped in to get the sand off. This time, I went to the public shower. We went back to the beach in July, and Paula and I sat there at sunset. Everyone else went back up to the beach house, and I sat out there for an hour and a half, looking out again at the water.

All the images came back, half-second glimpses of their faces and how the guys fought and what they said. It was awful. I tell someone this and they say, "Forget about it." I can't. I wish it were that easy. I lost three friends, including my best friend. They said their last words to me, and two of them died in my arms. Every time I look at the water, I get the same tormented feeling: My friends are still in there, and they'll always be in there.

Nick's Acknowledgments

Thanks to . . .

Mom, for being the main reason I held on. Words can never explain.

Paula, for taking care of me and never leaving my side. You have always put me first and for that I can't thank you enough. You are one in a billion.

My sister, Kris, for being as positive as you could have been and for always sticking by my side.

Dad, for supporting me though all of this. I know you're proud of me.

Bob, Betty, and Blake Bleakely for raising such an intelligent, respectful, and admirable son like Will who helped save my life. Losing my best friend has been traumatic, but I can't imagine what it's truly been like for you. I pray for you and thank you for your continuous love and support. Will has always spoken so highly of you. He loved you so much.

The Smith family, for having incredible faith and for sharing your words of encouragement with me. Corey had enough passion and faith for this lifetime and the next. Please continue to be strong for each other. I love you all and Corey.

The Cooper family, for creating such a strong-willed man who exemplified extreme dedication in everything he did: fishing, lifting, football, family. Marquis loved his family more than anything in this world. Your devotion to your son is extraordinary.

Rebekah, your undeniable faith has given me strength through some of my toughest moments. I admire you in so many ways, but mostly for being such an incredible parent to Goose. Delaney is incredibly blessed to have such wonderful parents. I pray that one day we can continue our friendship; it means more to me than you can imagine.

My family and the Oliveira family, for your continuous prayers, encouraging words, and constant support. I love you all.

To all of my friends, I cherish and love all of you. I am so grateful for all of you.

To everyone who visited me in the hospital or at home . . . Paul, Baidyr, Mark, Corey, John, Grant, Nick, Dave, Scott. Also thank you to all those who sent me cards and goodies.

Nate, Busbee, and Andy, I can't imagine getting through this without you. Thank you.

Ryan, Kenny, Pitt, Matt, and Tim for flying in to check in on me. To all my Lakewood brothers and Michael Marks, thanks for all the prayers.

Scott, I know how hard this has been for you. Stay strong. I love you, brother, and so does Will.

Thanks to my clients who have become great friends . . . Lori, Jan, Debbie, the Cetranglo family, the Franklin family, TC and Linda, the Howard Family, Julie, Mike Mpukarak, Mark and Amber, Andrea Tuggle, the Kravetz family, the Prokrana family, Rose, the Risavy family, Merle, Barb, Tracey, Joan, Jamie, the Darst family, the Nelson family.

My neighbors, Harry, Angie, Sheila, Chris, Noah, Alex, and Christopher.

My football friends on Saturday . . . thanks for the distraction and letting me feel fun again. One of the only times when I could think of something beside the accident. You all have no idea what this did for me.

USF Football Family, for your prayers.

Thank you to all my high school friends back north for sending love down south, especially the Smith family.

Thank you to everyone else who didn't even really know me for the prayers and encouragement through all of this. Whether it was the hundreds of cards or e-mail, it never go old.

Thank you to Jim Kelly, Tony Dungy, and Reverend Lane for your words of wisdom, and prayers as well.

My new family that has formed from all of this . . . my committee members from the Nick Schuyler Foundation. This amazing charity would never have been possible without all of you; Dina, Dean, Jane, Anita, and Lori. Along with all of the other volunteers and sponsors, thank you. I hope and believe that what we're doing is making my three fallen brothers proud.

Special thanks to Captain Tim Close and the Coast Guard. I can't say enough. Without you, I wouldn't have been given a second chance and an opportunity to tell this story.

Thanks to my agent Rick French, as well as Jack Glasure and the entire PR team at French/West/Vaughan for helping me through this difficult process.

Thanks to Dan Kelly and Fifth Year Productions for helping to make this book a reality.

Thank you to all the doctors and nurses and the hospital. You guys were amazing and spoiled me with kindness and endless Jell-O.

Thank you, Jeré, for helping me with this book and for being genuine.

Thank you most of all to my three fallen brothers: Will, Marquis, and Corey. I love and miss you all so very much! Even with this book, no one can fully understand what we went through out there at sea. I know you are watching down on us every day, protecting us. I know we will reunite once again. I know every day that you're dominating the football heavens. When you're not all catching touchdown passes and sacking quarterbacks, you're catching fish from heaven's seas. Fish way too big for this world.

I don't know why this happened to such amazing, loyal, and well-liked individuals. In a way I wish I was enjoying those days with you. But I do know the power of prayer, love, and friendship. Even though you're gone, we will always be together. I look forward to seeing you again. I love all of you.

Jeré's Acknowledgments

I'd like to thank Nick for the opportunity to help tell his story. And I'd like to offer my condolences to the families of Marquis, Corey, and Will. I know words can provide no consolation. The most we could offer was to make this book as accurate as possible.

I'd also like to thank Nick's family and Paula for assisting me. Captain Timothy Close and Lieutenant Bruno Baltazar of the St. Petersburg Coast Guard sector were greatly helpful in explaining search-and-rescue efforts. The crews of the cutter *Tornado*, led by Lieutenant Commander Patrick Peschka, and the airlifting Coast Guard helicopter patiently described their efforts to find and resuscitate Nick. The attending critical-care physician, Dr. Mark Rumbak of Tampa General Hospital, gave his time on a busy day to answer my medical questions. John Dunn of the hospital's public relations staff helped tremendously in cutting through the red tape.

Thanks to David Hirshey at HarperCollins for pitching my name and to Mauro DiPreta, my editor, whose diligence and sharp eye made this a smooth process at high speed. Special thanks to David Black, my agent, for his sage counsel, and Dave Larabell for his frequent and appreciated progress reports.

I am grateful to Tom Jolly, sports editor of the *New York Times,* and to Jason Stallman, assistant sports editor, for their support.

As always, this would not have been possible without the love, patience, and inexhaustible accommodation of Deborah, my wife, and Julie-Ann, our daughter.

Finally, to my dad. I love you and miss you.

Bibliography

Most of the source material for this book came from Nick Schuyler's recollection of what happened before, during, and after the tragic boating accident. We tried to confirm as much as we could in interviews with the Coast Guard, family members, and the doctor who treated Nick after he was rescued.

The official Coast Guard report of the case can be viewed at http://cgreport. wordpress.com/2009/03/21/the-search-and-rescue-of-nick-schuyler/

The official report of the Florida Fish and Wildlife Conservation Commission can be viewed at http://myfwc.com/docs/Newsroom/FWC_ACISS_%20BoatingAccidentInvestigativeReportFWSW_09_OFF.pdf

A number of newspaper and wire-service articles provided helpful information about the case and the lives and athletic careers of Nick, Will Bleakley, Marquis Cooper, and Corey Smith. We'd like to thank the Associated Press; Greg Auman, Lane DeGregory, and Erin Sullivan of the *St. Petersburg Times*; John Niyo and Bob Wojnowski of the *Detroit News*; Josh Slagter and Brian Van Ochten of the *Grand Rapids* (Mich.) *Press*; Steve Corkran of the *Contra Costa* (Calif.) *Times*; John McGrath of the *Tacoma* (Wash.) *News Tribune*; Mal Florence of the *Los Angeles Times*, and John Coscia of the *Citrus County* (Fla.) *Chronicle*.

http://www.tampabay.com/news/publicsafety/accidents/article980681.ece

http://www.dtf1.net/other-sports-teams-f22/lions-remember-lost-teammate-t4589.htm

http://sports.espn.go.com/nfl/news/story?id=4003668

http://www.mlive.com/lions/index.ssf/2009/03/spoiled_athlete_fomer_lion_cor.html

http://www.contracostatimes.com/raiders/ci_13848007?nclick_check=1

http://www.detroitnews.com/article/20090826/OPINION03/908260340

http://www.thenewstribune.com/sports/columnists/mcgrath/story/642763.html

http://articles.latimes.com/2002/oct/05/sports/sp-briefing5

http://www.tampabay.com/news/article982146.ece

http://www.tampabay.com/news/publicsafety/accidents/article980616.ece

http://blogs.tampabay.com/usf/2009/03/father-recalls.html

http://www.lcni5.com/cgi-bin/c2.cgi?071+article+News+20090304224639071311